Ineffective Assistance of Counsel Claims in North Carolina Criminal Cases

Jessica Smith

School of Government, UNC Chapel Hill

ESTABLISHED IN 1931, the Institute of Government provides training, advisory, and research services to public officials and others interested in the operation of state and local government in North Carolina. The Institute and the university's Master of Public Administration Program are the core activities of the School of Government at The University of North Carolina at Chapel Hill.

Each year approximately 14,000 public officials and others attend one or more of the more than 200 classes, seminars, and conferences offered by the Institute. Faculty members annually publish up to fifty books, bulletins, and other reference works related to state and local government. Each day that the General Assembly is in session, the Institute's *Daily Bulletin*, available in print and electronic format, reports on the day's activities for members of the legislature and others who need to follow the course of legislation. An extensive Web site (www.sog.unc.edu) provides access to publications and faculty research, course listings, program and service information, and links to other useful sites related to government.

Operating support for the School of Government's programs and activities comes from many sources, including state appropriations, local government membership dues, private contributions, publication sales, course fees, and service contracts. For more information about the School, the Institute, and the MPA program, visit the Web site or call (919) 966-5381.

Michael R. Smith, DEAN
Patricia A. Langelier, ASSOCIATE DEAN FOR OPERATIONS
Ann Cary Simpson, ASSOCIATE DEAN FOR DEVELOPMENT AND COMMUNICATIONS
Thomas H. Thornburg, ASSOCIATE DEAN FOR PROGRAMS
Ted D. Zoller, ASSOCIATE DEAN FOR BUSINESS AND FINANCE

FACULTY

Gregory S. Allison
Stephen Allred (on leave)
David N. Ammons
A. Fleming Bell, II
Maureen M. Berner
Frayda S. Bluestein
Mark F. Botts
Phillip Boyle
Joan G. Brannon
Mary Maureen Brown
Anita R. Brown-Graham
William A. Campbell
Anne M. Dellinger

James C. Drennan
Richard D. Ducker
Robert L. Farb
Joseph S. Ferrell
Milton S. Heath Jr.
Cheryl Daniels Howell
Joseph E. Hunt
Robert P. Joyce
Diane Juffras
David M. Lawrence
Ben F. Loeb Jr.
Janet Mason
Laurie L. Mesibov

Jill D. Moore
David W. Owens
William C. Rivenbark
John Rubin
John L. Saxon
Jessica Smith
John B. Stephens
A. John Vogt
Aimee Wall
Richard Whisnant
Gordon P. Whitaker

© 2003
School of Government
The University of North Carolina at Chapel Hill
⊗ This publication is printed on permanent, acid-free paper in compliance with the North Carolina General Statutes.
Printed in the United States of America

07 06 05 04 03 5 4 3 2 1

ISBN 1-56011-454-1
♻ Printed on recycled paper

Contents

Introduction

Ineffective assistance of counsel (IAC) claims are presented in state criminal cases in motions for appropriate relief (MARs) and on direct appeal. Additionally, issues regarding ineffectiveness can arise during the trial itself. Most commonly, the claims assert that the defendant was denied effective assistance of counsel because of attorney error, such as failing to object to evidence, call witnesses, or request a jury instruction. Attorney error claims are, however, only one category of IAC claims. Another category consists of denial of counsel claims. In this type of IAC claim, the defendant alleges that his or her right to effective assistance of counsel was violated because he or she was denied counsel at a critical stage of the criminal proceeding. An extreme example of such a claim is where the trial court refuses to appoint counsel to an indigent defendant faced with a felony charge. Another example is where the trial court allows the State to present inculpatory evidence against the defendant when defense counsel is absent from the courtroom. A third category of IAC claims consists of those that allege a denial of the right to effective assistance because counsel labored under a conflict of interest. One typical factual scenario falling in this class of claims is where one counsel represents two defendants, each of whom will present evidence exculpating himself or herself and inculpating the other. A final category includes claims where the defendant alleges that counsel was ineffective by making an unconsented-to admission of guilt. In North Carolina, these claims are called *Harbison* claims.

This book refers to all of these categories of claims as IAC claims. Although they are all grounded in the same constitutional provisions, different legal standards apply to the categories, complicating litigation and analysis. To facilitate litigation and resolution of IAC claims, this book begins by setting out the legal standards that apply to the different categories of IAC claims. It then goes on to offer a catalogue of published North Carolina appellate cases addressing IAC claims.[1] The catalogue

---

1. The catalogue includes criminal cases decided after the North Carolina Supreme Court's decision in *State v. Braswell*, 312 N.C. 553, 324 S.E.2d 241 (1985). In *Braswell*, the North Carolina Supreme Court adopted the federal IAC standard, as set forth in *Strickland v. Washington*, 466 U.S. 668 (1984), for IAC claims alleging that attorney error resulted in a violation of state constitutional rights.

is divided into categories of specific allegations of ineffectiveness, arranged to roughly track the order of a criminal trial. It begins with cases in which the defendant
alleged ineffectiveness in the pretrial stages of a criminal case, moves on to cases
in which the defendant alleged ineffectiveness at trial, and then covers cases in which
the defendant alleged ineffectiveness on appeal. Although IAC claims are often fact
dependent, the catalogue is designed to serve as a benchmark for judges when ruling on such claims. Further guidance can be found in the literature summarizing
the many federal IAC cases.[2]

---

2. *See, e.g.*, WAYNE LAFAVE, JEROLD ISRAEL & NANCY KING, 3 CRIMINAL PROCEDURE §§ 11.7–11.10
(2d ed. 1999); JAMES LIEBMAN & RANDY HERTZ, 1 FEDERAL HABEAS CORPUS PRACTICE & PROCEDURE
§ 11.2c(13) (3d ed. 1998).

Part I: The Legal Standards

§ 1.01   Constitutional Bases

The constitutional bases for most IAC claims raised in the North Carolina courts are the Sixth Amendment to the United States Constitution, made applicable to the states through the Fourteenth Amendment,[1] and Article I, Sections 19 and 23, of the North Carolina Constitution.[2]

The Sixth Amendment provides, in relevant part, that "[i]n all criminal prosecutions the accused shall . . . have the assistance of counsel for his defense." Article I, Section 23, of the North Carolina Constitution contains an almost identical provision.[3] The standard for evaluating claims based on the North Carolina Constitution mirrors the standard for evaluating claims based on the Sixth Amendment to the federal Constitution.[4]

---

1. *See* Gideon v. Wainwright, 372 U.S. 335, 342 (1963).

2. *See* State v. James, 111 N.C. App. 785, 789, 433 S.E.2d 755, 757 (1993) (right to counsel guaranteed by the Sixth Amendment is made applicable to the states through the Fourteenth Amendment and §§ 19 and 23 of the North Carolina Constitution). Additionally, defendants have limited equal protection and due process rights to the assistance of counsel. For a detailed discussion of the scope of these rights, see WAYNE LAFAVE, JEROLD ISRAEL & NANCY KING, 3 CRIMINAL PROCEDURE §§ 11.1(b) & (d) (2d ed. 1999) [herinafter LAFAVE]. Most significantly, due process requires a right to counsel for a first appeal of right. *See id.* § 11.1(b), at 473.

3. N.C. CONST. art. I, § 23 ("In all criminal prosecutions, every person . . . has the right . . . to have counsel for defense. . . .").

4. *See* State v. Braswell, 312 N.C. 553, 324 S.E.2d 241 (1985); *see also* State v. McMillian, 147 N.C. App. 707, 557 S.E.2d 138, 144 (2001) ("The test for [IAC] is the same under the federal and state constitutions."), *review denied*, 355 N.C. 219, 560 S.E.2d 152 (2002). In *Braswell*, the North Carolina Supreme Court adopted the federal IAC standard, as set forth in *Strickland v. Washington*, 466 U.S. 668 (1984), for IAC claims alleging that attorney error resulted in a violation of state constitutional rights. *See Braswell*, 312 N.C. at 562–63, 324 S.E.2d at 248 ("[W]e expressly adopt the test set out in *Strickland v. Washington* as a uniform

The Sixth Amendment guarantees not only the right to assistance of counsel, but also the right to *effective* assistance of counsel.[5] Broadly defined, the right to effective assistance of counsel is "the right of the accused to require the prosecution's case to survive the crucible of meaningful adversarial testing."[6] The sections that follow flesh out the relevant standards for determining whether the constitutional right to effective assistance of counsel has been violated.

§ 1.02   Scope of the Right to Effective Assistance of Counsel

A preliminary determination for any IAC claim is whether the defendant had a constitutional right to counsel at the time of the alleged ineffectiveness. If there is no right to counsel, then there can be no violation of the constitutional right to effective assistance of counsel.[7] In order to determine whether a defendant has a Sixth Amendment right to counsel at the time of the alleged ineffectiveness, the decision maker must ask a three-part question: whether the Sixth Amendment covers (1) the counsel alleged to be ineffective, (2) the proceeding at which the ineffectiveness allegedly occurred, and (3) the particular offense. If any part of this question is answered in the negative, the IAC claim fails to meet the threshold requirement that the defendant has a Sixth Amendment right to counsel, and the claim must be denied. If all of the parts are answered in the affirmative, the claim must be analyzed under the appropriate IAC standard.[8] The sections that follow explore the requisite inquiries. Of course, the right

---

standard to be applied to measure [IAC] under the North Carolina Constitution."). The North Carolina courts have, without discussion, applied to IAC claims asserted under the state constitution the alternate IAC standards that have developed under federal law. *See, e.g., infra* § 1.05[2][d] (citing and discussing North Carolina cases applying the federal constitutional standard for conflict of interest claims stated in *Cuyler v. Sullivan,* 446 U.S. 335 (1980)).

5. *See* Strickland v. Washington, 466 U.S. 668, 686 (1984) ("'the right to counsel is the right to the effective assistance of counsel'") (quoting McMann v. Richardson, 397 U.S. 759, 771 n.14 (1970)); United States v. Cronic, 466 U.S. 648, 654 (1984) (same); *Braswell,* 312 N.C. at 561, 324 S.E.2d at 247 (1985) (same). In *Evitts v. Lucey,* 469 U.S. 387 (1985), the United States Supreme Court acknowledged that its earlier cases held that the trial-level right to counsel "comprehends the right to effective assistance of counsel." *Id.* at 392 (citing *Gideon,* 372 U.S. 335; Cuyler v. Sullivan, 446 U.S. 335 (1980)). *Evitts* went on to hold that "the appellate-level right to counsel also comprehends the right to effective assistance." *Id.* at 392, 396.

6. *Cronic,* 466 U.S. at 656.

7. *See* Wainwright v. Torna, 455 U.S. 586, 587–88 (1982) ("[s]ince respondent had no constitutional right to counsel, he could not be deprived of the effective assistance of counsel"); *Evitts,* 469 U.S. at 397 n.7 ("Of course, the right to effective assistance of counsel is dependent on the right to counsel itself."); LaFave, *supra* note 2, § 11.7(a), at 616 ("where there is no constitutional right to the assistance of counsel . . . there does not exist a constitutional right to effective representation by counsel").

8. *See infra* pp. 15–57 (setting out the standards that apply to the various categories of IAC claims).

to counsel may be waived. Thus, even if a defendant had a Sixth Amendment right to counsel, the defendant's IAC claim will fail if he or she knowingly, voluntarily, and intelligently waived that right.[9]

[1] Covered Counsel

The Sixth Amendment applies to both retained and appointed counsel.[10] However, two categories of counsel fall outside of the Sixth Amendment's protections. First, the North Carolina Supreme Court has held that although an indigent defendant has the *statutory* right to the appointment of additional counsel in capital cases,[11] a defendant has no *constitutional* right to the assistance of such counsel.[12] Thus, under North Carolina law, a capital defendant cannot successfully base a constitutional IAC claim on the role of additional counsel.[13] Second, the federal circuit courts of appeals have held that

---

9. *See infra* note 206 (discussing waiver).

10. *See Cuyler*, 446 U.S. at 334 ("A proper respect for the Sixth Amendment disarms [the prosecution's] contention that defendants who retain their own counsel are entitled to less protection than defendants for whom the State appoints counsel."); Mickens v. Taylor, 122 S. Ct. 1237, 1242 n.2 (2002) (quoting *Cuyler*); *Evitts*, 469 U.S. at 395 ("the constitutional guarantee of effective assistance of counsel at trial applies to every criminal prosecution, without regard to whether counsel is retained or appointed"). *See generally* LaFave, *supra* note 2, § 11.7(b), at 620 & n.27 (discussing *Cuyler* and citing later-decided decisions of the lower federal courts that have "uniformly held that the standard of review applied to all types of ineffectiveness claims will not vary with the status of counsel as retained or court-appointed").

11. *See* N.C. Gen. Stat. § 7A-450(b1) (hereinafter G.S.) ("An indigent person indicted for murder may not be tried where the State is seeking the death penalty without an assistant counsel being appointed in a timely manner. If the indigent person is represented by the public defender's office, the requirement of an assistant counsel may be satisfied by the assignment to the case of an additional attorney from the public defender's staff.").

12. *See* State v. Locklear, 322 N.C. 349, 357, 368 S.E.2d 377, 382 (1988).

13. *See id.* (rejecting defendant's claim that the trial court erred by not acting *ex mero motu* to continue a hearing on certain pretrial motions so that his court-appointed counsel could have "adequate time" to confer with retained counsel and stating: "An indigent defendant's right to the appointment of *additional* counsel in capital cases is statutory, not constitutional. Defendant thus has no *constitutional* right to the assistance of such counsel, in the hearing of his motions or otherwise.") (citation omitted); *see also* State v. Call, 353 N.C. 400, 413–15, 545 S.E.2d 190, 199–200 (2001) (rejecting defendant's argument that the trial court violated his right to effective assistance of counsel by permitting only one of his attorneys to object during the prosecutor's examination of a witness; citing *Locklear* and holding that even if this constitutional argument had been preserved, it would fail because an indigent defendant's right to additional counsel in capital cases is statutory, not constitutional), *cert. denied*, 122 S. Ct. 628 (2001); State v. Frye, 341 N.C. 470, 492–93, 461 S.E.2d 664, 674–75 (1995) (same). A defendant may be able to argue that by creating a statutory right to additional counsel in capital cases, the General Assembly contemplated that such counsel would satisfy the standard of effectiveness that applies to Sixth Amendment counsel. However, such an argument is based on statutory rights, not the Sixth Amendment, and as such is beyond the scope of this book.

the Sixth Amendment right to effective assistance of counsel does not apply to stand-by counsel appointed to a defendant who has properly exercised his or her right to self-representation.[14] However, in North Carolina, a decision by the state supreme court may suggest that the door has not been closed entirely to a claim asserting IAC with respect to standby counsel. In *State v. Thomas*,[15] the North Carolina Supreme Court held that the trial court committed reversible error by allowing the defendant to represent himself at his capital murder trial. In the course of its holding, the court reviewed the law regarding standby counsel and stated: "Because 'standby counsel' is a creature of legislation, with duties limited by statute, defendant does not benefit from a typical lawyer-client relationship. He thus cannot claim ineffective assistance on the part of standby counsel beyond the limited scope of the duties assigned to such counsel by the statute or the defendant or voluntarily assumed by such counsel."[16] This dictum suggests that there may be viability for a claim that standby counsel was ineffective with respect to duties assigned by the statute or the defendant or voluntarily assumed by standby counsel. The dictum is, however, inconsistent with the North Carolina Supreme Court's holding in *State v. Locklear*.[17] In that case, the court held that a defendant has no constitutional right to additional counsel in a capital case. *Locklear* draws a clear distinction between a statutory right to counsel and a constitutional right to counsel. This fact, along with the ample federal authority holding that an IAC claim cannot be asserted under the Sixth Amendment with regard to standby counsel, suggests that the *Thomas* dictum is not likely to be adopted as constitutional law.

Not surprisingly, if a defendant knowingly and intelligently elects to proceed pro se, he or she cannot later assert an IAC claim.[18]

[2]   Covered Proceedings
[a]   Trial

The second step in determining whether there is a Sixth Amendment right to counsel is determining whether the particular proceeding is covered by the Sixth Amendment.

---

14. *See, e.g.*, United States v. Lawrence, 161 F.3d 250, 253 (4th Cir. 1998) ("The Sixth Amendment does not require a court to grant advisory counsel to a criminal defendant who chooses to exercise his right to self-representation by proceeding *pro se*."); United States v. Schmidt, 105 F.3d 82, 90 (2d Cir. 1997) (no constitutional right to hybrid representation; "[a]bsent a constitutional right to standby counsel, a defendant generally cannot prove standby counsel was ineffective").

15. 331 N.C. 671, 417 S.E.2d 473 (1992).

16. 331 N.C. at 677, 417 S.E.2d at 478.

17. 322 N.C. 349, 368 S.E.2d 377 (1988).

18. *See* Faretta v. California, 422 U.S. 806, 834 n.46 (1975) ("a defendant who elects to represent himself cannot thereafter complain that the quality of his own defense amounted to a denial of 'effective assistance of counsel'"); *Thomas*, 331 N.C. at 677, 417 S.E.2d at 477 ("if a defendant chooses to proceed pro se, he cannot on appeal claim [IAC]"). For a case addressing a defendant's claim that standby counsel's unsolicited participation violated his right to proceed pro se, see *McKaskle v. Wiggins*, 465 U.S. 168, (1984).

This inquiry examines the scope of the *constitutional right* to counsel, which must be distinguished from any *statutorily created rights* to counsel.[19]

By its terms, the Sixth Amendment applies only to "criminal prosecutions."[20] Criminal contempt proceedings qualify as criminal prosecutions.[21] Although there is no case law on point in North Carolina, other jurisdictions have held that civil forfeiture proceedings fall outside the scope of the Sixth Amendment's right to counsel.[22]

The term "criminal prosecutions," as used in the Sixth Amendment, includes all critical stages of the criminal trial.[23] The inquiry into whether a particular stage is a critical one focuses on "whether potential substantial prejudice to defendant's rights inheres in the . . . confrontation and the ability of counsel to help avoid that prejudice."[24] Unless there is controlling case law on point, this inquiry must be made on a case-by-case basis.[25]

---

19. In North Carolina, the General Assembly has, by statute, extended an indigent defendant's right to counsel to proceedings not covered by the Sixth Amendment. *Compare* G.S. 7A-451(a)(3) (extending right to counsel to certain motions for appropriate relief) *with* Pennsylvania v. Finley, 481 U.S. 551, 555 (1987) (holding that the Sixth Amendment right to counsel extends to the first appeal as of right "and no further"). A discussion of these statutorily created rights is beyond the scope of this book.

20. U.S. Const. amend. VI; *see* State v. Adams, 345 N.C. 745, 748, 483 S.E.2d 156, 157 (1997) ("By its terms, the Sixth Amendment applies only to criminal cases."); *see also* Sanchez v. United States Postal Serv., 785 F.2d 1236, 1237 (5th Cir. 1986); Wolfolk v. Rivera, 729 F.2d 1114, 1120–21 (7th Cir. 1984); Allen v. Barnes Hosp., 721 F.2d 643, 644 (8th Cir. 1983); Mekdeci v. Merrell National Lab., 711 F.2d 1510, 1522–23 (11th Cir. 1983).

21. *See* 8B James W. Moore, Moore's Federal Practice ¶ 42.02[2] (2d ed. 1996) ("Criminal contempt proceedings . . . require such protections as the sixth amendment right to counsel. . . .").

22. *See, e.g.*, United States v. 87 Blackheath Rd., 201 F.3d 98, 99 (2d Cir. 2000) (citing cases from other circuits). Some state courts have followed suit, finding no right to counsel in forfeiture proceedings. *See, e.g.*, People v. Cobb, 944 P.2d 574, 576–77 (Colo. App. 1996) (citing federal cases).

A separate but related issue is whether a defendant's Sixth Amendment right to counsel is violated when a court enters an order freezing assets that the defendant wishes to use to pay an attorney to represent him or her in a criminal proceeding that is covered by the Sixth Amendment. Interpreting the federal Constitution, the United States Supreme Court has answered this question in the negative. *See* Caplin & Drysdale Chartered v. United States, 491 U.S. 617 (1989). Interpreting its state constitution, at least one state court has concluded otherwise. *See* Commonwealth v. Hess, 617 A.2d 307, 315 (Pa. 1992) (state forfeiture statute violates state constitution insofar as it applies to the payment of attorney's fees for legitimate criminal defense representation prior to conviction).

23. *See* Gideon v. Wainwright, 372 U.S. 335 (1963) (right to assistance of counsel at state felony trials). As noted above, other constitutional provisions create a right to counsel for first appeals of right. *See supra* note 2.

24. Coleman v. Alabama, 399 U.S. 1, 9 (1970) (quoting United States v. Wade, 388 U.S. 218, 227 (1967)).

25. *Cf.* Hamilton v. Alabama, 368 U.S. 52, 53–54 & n.4 (1961) (holding that under Alabama law, an arraignment is a critical stage because available defenses "may

The following trial stages are among those that have been held to be critical:

- jury selection,[26]
- presentation of inculpatory evidence,[27]
- presentation of the defendant's testimony,[28]
- closing argument in jury and nonjury cases,[29]
- sentencing,[30] and
- a post-trial, pre-appeal motion for a new trial.[31]

be as irretrievably lost, if not then and there asserted, as they are when an accused represented by counsel waives a right for strategic purposes" but noting that arraignment "has differing consequences in the various jurisdictions"); State v. Hall, 39 N.C. App. 728, 732, 252 S.E.2d 100, 103 (1979) ("what constitutes a critical stage is determined both from the nature of the proceedings and from the facts in each case").

26. *See* State v. Colbert, 311 N.C. 283, 285, 316 S.E.2d. 79, 80 (1984); *see also* United States v. Hanno, 21 F.3d 42, 47 (4th Cir. 1994).

Not every single stage of jury selection is critical. In *State v. Roper*, 328 N.C. 337, 402 S.E.2d 600 (1991), the trial judge determined that the venire pool was too small and ordered that additional venire persons be selected at random from an array present for the trial of other cases in an adjoining courtroom. The jurors from the adjoining room already had been sworn but had not been impaneled or selected for another case. The defendant argued that this action violated his right to effective assistance, apparently on grounds that counsel was not present when the jurors were sworn in the other courtroom. The court rejected this argument, concluding that the jurors "were merely sworn by another judge in another courtroom" and that there "was no possibility" that defendant's rights were compromised. 328 N.C. at 355, 402 S.E.2d at 610.

27. *See* Burdine v. Johnson, 262 F.3d 336, 347–48 (5th Cir. 2001) (holding that the guilt–innocence phase of capital trial where evidence was produced against defendant was a critical stage), *cert. denied*, 122 S. Ct. 2347 (2002); Olden v. United States, 224 F.3d 561, 568 (6th Cir. 2000); United States v. Russell, 205 F.3d 768, 772 (5th Cir. 2000) (government's presentation of evidence against co-conspirators in counsel's absence). That portion of trial where no inculpatory evidence has been presented has been held by one federal circuit court not to be a critical stage. *See* Vines v. United States, 28 F.3d 1123, 1128 (11th Cir. 1994) (holding in a multi-defendant case that because no evidence directly inculpating defendant was presented during counsel's absence, stage was not critical and presumption of prejudice was unwarranted).

28. *See* Ferguson v. Georgia, 365 U.S. 570, 596 (1961) (State cannot deny defendant the right to have defense counsel elicit defendant's testimony through direct examination).

29. *See* Herring v. New York, 422 U.S. 853, 858 (1975).

30. *See* Gardner v. Florida, 430 U.S. 349, 358 (1977) (in a capital case, considering the constitutionality of a trial judge's use of a confidential pre-sentence report, the Court noted that "sentencing is a critical stage of the criminal proceeding at which [defendant] is entitled to the effective assistance of counsel"); State v. Strickland, 318 N.C. 653, 660, 351 S.E.2d 281, 285 (1987) ("We agree with the Court of Appeals that sentencing is a critical stage of a criminal proceeding to which the right to effective assistance of counsel applies") (quotation omitted); State v. Lambert, 146 N.C. App. 360, 363, 553 S.E.2d 71, 75 (2001) ("Sentencing is a critical stage of the criminal proceeding during which the criminal defendant is entitled to effective assistance of counsel."), *review denied* by 355 N.C. 289, 561 S.E.2d 271 (2002); State v. Davidson, 77 N.C. App. 540, 544, 335 S.E.2d 518, 521 (1985) (same).

31. *See* Kitchen v. United States, 227 F.3d 1014, 1018–19 (7th Cir. 2000).

Although courts in other jurisdictions have held that resentencing is a critical trial stage,[32] in *State v. Lambert*,[33] the North Carolina Court of Appeals held that the right to counsel does not apply at resentencing when the trial court is not likely to sentence the defendant to an active term of imprisonment. In *Lambert*, the defendant was convicted of the unauthorized practice of law. He contended on appeal after resentencing that the trial court violated his rights by failing to appoint counsel for the resentencing. At the original sentencing, the defendant received a suspended sentence with regular and special conditions of probation. On the defendant's first appeal, the court of appeals found no error in the trial. The court vacated in part and remanded for resentencing, however, finding that the trial court had erred in delegating a judicial function to the defendant's probation officer by including a special condition of probation that defendant not file documents in any court without prior approval from his probation officer. At resentencing, the only issue addressed by the trial court was modification of this special condition. In the second appeal, the court of appeals held that the resentencing hearing was not a critical stage of the criminal proceedings, noting the limited nature of the trial court's inquiry and the fact that the trial court was not likely to sentence the defendant to an active term of imprisonment.[34] *Lambert* is questionable in light of the United States Supreme Court's later holding in *Alabama v. Shelton*[35] that a suspended sentence may not be imposed on an uncounseled defendant absent a valid waiver of counsel.[36]

The federal circuit courts have held that some trial stages are not critical ones.[37] Two of the trial stages that these courts have found not to be critical are the State's presentation of noninculpatory evidence[38] and pre-sentence interviews.[39]

---

32. *See, e.g.*, Hall v. Moore, 253 F.3d 624, 628 (11th Cir. 2001) (trial court's actions on resentencing were not merely "ministerial").

33. 146 N.C. App. 360, 553 S.E.2d 71.

34. *See infra* p. 14 (discussing the actual imprisonment standard for misdemeanor offenses covered by the Sixth Amendment).
    The *Lambert* court concluded: "[W]e determine that none of the defendant's constitutional rights were violated during resentencing because under . . . [G.S.] § 7A–451, defendant was not entitled to counsel." *See Lambert*, 146 N.C. App. at 364–65, 553 S.E.2d at 75. This statement erroneously suggests that the determination of whether a constitutional right to counsel exists turns on whether the State has a statutorily created right to counsel in this context. *See supra* p. 5 (distinguishing between constitutional rights and statutorily created rights).

35. 122 S. Ct. 1764 (2002).

36. *See infra* p. 14 (discussing *Alabama*).

37. *But see* State v. Colbert, 311 N.C. 283, 316 S.E.2d 79 (1984) (holding that defendant's right to counsel was violated when jury selection proceeded in counsel's absence; stating in dictum that "[d]efendant's right to counsel extends to the entire trial").

38. *See* Vines v. United States, 28 F.3d 1123, 1128 (11th Cir. 1994) ("where . . . no evidence directly inculpating a defendant is presented while that defendant's counsel is absent, we decline to hold that counsel was absent during a critical stage of the trial").

39. *See* United States v. Benlian, 63 F.3d 824, 827 (9th Cir. 1995) (citing similar cases from several other circuits).

[b]   Pretrial
[i]   When the Sixth Amendment Right Attaches

The Sixth Amendment right to counsel attaches only at or after the initiation of adversary judicial proceedings, whether by formal charge, preliminary hearing, indictment, information, or arraignment.[40] The United States Supreme Court has explained:

> The initiation of judicial proceedings is far from a mere formalism. It is the starting point of our whole system of adversary criminal justice. For it is only then that the government has committed itself to prosecute, and only then that the adverse positions of government and defendant have solidified. It is then that a defendant finds himself faced with the prosecutorial forces of organized society, and immersed in the intricacies of substantive and procedural criminal law. It is this point, therefore, that marks the commencement of the "criminal prosecutions" to which alone the explicit guarantees of the Sixth Amendment are applicable.[41]

Thus, a bright-line rule applies to the issue of whether the Sixth Amendment right to counsel has attached: The right does not apply until adversary judicial proceedings have been initiated, whether by formal charge, preliminary hearing, indictment, information, or arraignment. Arrest or issuance of an arrest warrant does not constitute initiation of adversary judicial proceedings.[42] Nor does a Department of Social Services petition alleging abuse and neglect constitute initiation of adversary judicial

---

40. *See* Kirby v. Illinois, 406 U.S. 682, 688 (1972) ("it has been firmly established that a person's Sixth and Fourteenth Amendment right to counsel attaches only at or after the time that adversary proceedings have been initiated against him"); State v. Taylor, 354 N.C. 28, 35, 550 S.E.2d 141, 147 (2001) ("As we have said previously, a defendant's right to counsel under the Sixth and Fourteenth Amendments attaches only at such time as adversary judicial proceedings have been instituted whether by way of formal charge, preliminary hearing, indictment, information or arraignment.") (quotations omitted), *cert. denied*, 122 S. Ct. 1312 (2002); State v. Warren, 348 N.C. 80, 95, 499 S.E.2d 431, 439 (1998) (same); State v. Phipps, 331 N.C. 427, 441, 418 S.E.2d 178, 185 (1992) (same); State v. Nations, 319 N.C. 318, 324, 354 S.E.2d 510, 513 (1987) (same).

41. *Kirby*, 406 U.S. at 689–90.

42. *See* United States v. Gouveia, 467 U.S. 180, 190 (1984) ("we have never held that the right to counsel attaches at the time of arrest"); *Taylor*, 354 N.C. at 36, 550 S.E.2d at 147 ("An arrest warrant for first-degree murder is not a sufficient charging document upon which a defendant can be tried. Therefore, an arrest warrant for first-degree murder in this state is not a formal charge. . . . Defendant's Sixth Amendment right to counsel did not attach either at the issuance of the warrant or at the time of his arrest upon the warrant. . . ."); State v. Gibbs, 335 N.C. 1, 43, 436 S.E.2d 321, 345 (1993) (rejecting defendant's argument that a Sixth Amendment right to counsel attached when he was arrested); State v. Stokes, 150 N.C. App. 211, 220, 565 S.E.2d 196, 202–03 (2001) (rejecting defendant's argument that his right to counsel attached because he had been served with a warrant charging him with murder and he had been arrested and had appeared before a magistrate), *cert. denied*, 356 N.C. 175, 569 S.E.2d 277, *review on additional issues allowed in part by* 356 N.C. 175, 569 S.E.2d 278 (2002).

proceedings.[43] In the absence of an indictment, the North Carolina Supreme Court has held that the right to counsel attaches at first appearance.[44]

In *Escobedo v. Illinois*,[45] the United States Supreme Court deviated from this bright-line rule. In *Escobedo*, the defendant was taken into custody before being charged, was interrogated, and made incriminating statements to the police. During the interrogation, the defendant repeatedly requested to speak with his attorney and his attorney repeatedly asked to speak with the defendant. These requests were denied. The Court found that the defendant's Sixth Amendment right was violated, stating:

> [W]here . . . the investigation is no longer a general inquiry into an unsolved crime but has begun to focus on a particular suspect, the suspect has been taken into custody, the police carry out a process of interrogations that lends itself to eliciting incriminating statements, the suspect has requested and has been denied an opportunity to consult with his lawyer, and the police have not effectively warned him of his . . . right to remain silent, the accused has been denied "the Assistance of Counsel" in violation of the Sixth Amendment.[46]

The *Escobedo* Court thus applied the Sixth Amendment's right to counsel protections to a suspect in a precharge interrogation—that is, before initiation of adversary judicial proceedings. Later Supreme Court cases, however, "foreclose any reliance on *Escobedo* . . . for the proposition that the Sixth Amendment . . . applies prior to the initiation of adversary judicial proceedings."[47] Specifically, the Court has stated that although *Escobedo* was decided as a Sixth Amendment case, it has been viewed in retrospect as a self-incrimination case.[48] Additionally, the case has been strictly limited to its facts and remains a lone Supreme Court exception to the bright-line rule that the Sixth Amendment does not attach until initiation of adversary judicial proceedings.[49]

---

43. *See* State v. Adams, 345 N.C. 745, 748, 483 S.E.2d 156, 156 (1997) ("The filing of a petition alleging abuse and neglect commences a civil proceeding. By its terms, the Sixth Amendment applies only to criminal cases.").

44. *See Gibbs*, 335 N.C. at 44, 436 S.E.2d at 345 ("Although the first appearance itself is not a critical stage of criminal judicial proceedings at which a defendant is entitled to counsel, we conclude defendant's Sixth Amendment right to counsel attached during his first appearance.") (citation omitted); State v. Bromfield, 332 N.C. 24, 39, 418 S.E.2d 491, 499 (1992) ("defendant's right to counsel attached at his first appearance").

45. 378 U.S. 478 (1964).

46. *Id*. at 490–91. The Court clarified that its holding only applies "when the process shifts from investigatory to accusatory—when its focus is on the accused and its purpose is to elicit a confession." *Id*. at 492.

47. Moran v. Burbine, 475 U.S. 412, 429 (1986).

48. *Id*. at 429–30 ("Although *Escobedo* was originally decided as a Sixth Amendment case, the Court in retrospect perceived the prime purpose of *Escobedo* was not to vindicate the constitutional right to counsel as such but, like *Miranda*, to guarantee full effectuation of the privilege against self-incrimination.") (quotations omitted).

49. *See* Kirby v. Illinois, 406 U.S. 682, 689 (1972) (noting that *Escobedo* has been limited to its own facts and refusing to hold that the Sixth Amendment applied to a police station show-up that occurred before defendant had been indicted or otherwise formally charged

[ii]   Covered Pretrial Proceedings

The Sixth Amendment right to counsel is not limited to the right to counsel at trial.[50] Defendants are guaranteed that they "'need not stand alone against the State at any stage of the prosecution, formal or informal, in court or out, where counsel's absence might derogate from the accused's right to a fair trial.'"[51] Once the Sixth Amendment attaches, it extends to "critical stages of the proceedings," including all critical pretrial proceedings. The determination of whether a particular pretrial proceeding is critical requires application of the same test applied to determine whether a particular trial proceeding is critical: "whether potential substantial prejudice to defendant's rights inheres in the particular confrontation and the ability of counsel to help avoid that prejudice."[52]

Applying this test, the United States Supreme Court has held that a pretrial arraignment where certain rights may be sacrificed or lost is a critical stage.[53] North Carolina's arraignment is such a procedure, and the state courts have held it to be a critical stage at which the defendant has a constitutional right to counsel.[54]

In *Coleman v. Alabama*,[55] the United States Supreme Court held that Alabama's preliminary hearing is a critical stage in the proceeding.[56] Noting that the relevant inquiry was whether potential substantial prejudice to the defendant's rights inheres in the confrontation and the ability of counsel to help avoid that prejudice, the Court held that "[p]lainly the guiding hand of counsel at the preliminary hearing is essential to protect the indigent accused against an erroneous or improper prosecution."[57] It explained:

> First, the lawyer's skilled examination and cross-examination of witnesses may expose fatal weaknesses in the State's case that may lead the magistrate to refuse to bind the

---

with a crime); *Moran*, 475 U.S. at 429–32 (rejecting defendant's contention that his Sixth Amendment rights were violated prior to formal initiation of adversary judicial proceedings); *see also* State v. Detter, 298 N.C. 604, 621, 260 S.E.2d 567, 580 (1979) (noting that the Supreme Court has limited *Escobedo*).

50. *See Kirby*, 406 U.S. at 688 ("This is not to say that a defendant in a criminal case has a constitutional right to counsel only at the trial itself."); *Detter*, 298 N.C. at 619, 260 S.E.2d at 579 ("[T]he right to counsel attaches and applies not only at trial but also at and after any pretrial proceeding that is determined to constitute a critical stage.").

51. Coleman v. Alabama, 399 U.S. 1, 7 (1970) (quoting United States v. Wade, 388 U.S. 218, 226 (1967)).

52. *Id.* at 7; *Detter*, 298 N.C. at 620, 260 S.E.2d at 579 (same); *see supra* p. 5 (discussing this test in terms of trial stages).

53. *See* Hamilton v. Alabama, 368 U.S. 52, 54 (1961) (holding that "[w]hatever may be the function and importance of arraignment in other jurisdictions," arraignment in Alabama is a critical stage because "[a]vailable defenses may be as irretrievably lost, if not then and there asserted, as they are when an accused represented by counsel waives a right for strategic purposes") (footnote omitted).

54. *See* State v. Pait, 81 N.C. App. 286, 290, 343 S.E.2d 573, 576 (1986) ("A criminal defendant is entitled to the assistance of counsel at all critical stages of the criminal trial process, including arraignment.").

55. 399 U.S. 1 (1970).

56. *See id.* at 9–10.

57. *Id.* at 9.

Table 1: Critical Pretrial Proceedings

Arraignment where rights may be sacrificed or lost[a]
Plea proceedings[b]
Preliminary hearing/probable cause hearing[c]
Post-indictment, pretrial lineups[d]
Police interrogation after initiation of adversarial proceedings[e]

---

a. *See* Hamilton v. Alabama, 368 U.S. 52, 54 (1961).

b. *See Detter*, 298 N.C. at 619, 260 S.E.2d at 579 ("The right to counsel applies at the taking of a guilty plea.").

c. *See* Coleman v. Alabama, 399 U.S. 1, 9–10 (1970); White v. Maryland, 373 U.S. 59, 60 (1963); *Detter*, 298 N.C. 604, 260 S.E.2d 567.

d. *See* United States v. Wade, 388 U.S. 218, 237 (1967) (post-indictment pretrial identification lineup was a critical stage of criminal proceedings at which the Sixth Amendment right to counsel was applicable); State v. Connally, 36 N.C. App. 43, 47–48, 243 S.E.2d 788, 791 (1978); State v. Davis, 33 N.C. App. 736, 739, 236 S.E.2d 722, 724 (1977).

e. *See* Massiah v. United States, 377 U.S. 201, 206 (1964) (surreptitious interrogation); Michigan v. Jackson, 475 U.S. 625, 629–30 (1986); State v. Tucker, 331 N.C. 12, 33, 414 S.E.2d 548, 560 (1992). Of course, defendants have a Fifth Amendment right to counsel at custodial interrogations, regardless of when those interrogations occur. *See* Miranda v. Arizona, 384 U.S. 436 (1966).

---

accused over. Second, in any event, the skilled interrogation of witnesses by an experienced lawyer can fashion a vital impeachment tool for use in cross-examination of the State's witnesses at the trial, or preserve testimony favorable to the accused of a witness who does not appear at the trial. Third, trained counsel can more effectively discover the case the State has against his client and make possible the preparation of a proper defense to meet that case at the trial. Fourth, counsel can also be influential at the preliminary hearing in making effective arguments for the accused on such matters as the necessity for an early psychiatric examination or bail.

The inability of the indigent accused on his own to realize these advantages of a lawyer's assistance compels the conclusion that the Alabama preliminary hearing is a "critical stage" of the State's criminal process at which the accused is "as much entitled to such aid (of counsel) as at the trial itself."[58]

North Carolina's probable cause hearing is the functional equivalent of the preliminary hearing at issue in *Coleman*.[59] Not surprisingly, the North Carolina Supreme Court has held that such hearings are critical stages.[60]

Table 1 lists these and other pretrial proceedings that the United States Supreme Court and the North Carolina courts have held to be critical pretrial stages of the proceeding to which the Sixth Amendment applies.

---

58. *Id.* at 9–10 (quoting Powell v. Alabama, 287 U.S. 45, 57 (1932)).

59. *See* G.S. 15A-611 & 15A-612 (probable cause hearing procedure).

60. *See* State v. Detter, 298 N.C. 604, 624, 260 S.E.2d 567, 582 (1979) ("the probable cause hearing is a critical stage triggering application of the Sixth Amendment right to counsel") (citing State v. Cobb, 295 N.C. 1, 243 S.E.2d 759 (1978)).

Table 2: Noncritical Pretrial Proceedings

Taking of handwriting exemplars[a]
Taking of blood samples[b]
Taking of fingerprints, clothing, hair, and voice demonstrations[c]
Administration of a chemical analysis to determine if a driver is under the influence of an impairing substance[d]
Precharge show-up,[e] lineup,[f] or other precharge identification, whether in person[g] or by photograph[h]
Administration of a gunshot residue test[i]
Competency evaluation[j]
Judicial hearing on probable cause for pretrial detention[k]
First appearance[l]
Trial judge's announcement of ruling regarding release of prison records to the prosecution[m]

a. *See* Gilbert v. California, 388 U.S. 263, 267 (1967); State v. Carson, 296 N.C. 31, 38, 249 S.E.2d 417, 422 (1978).

b. *See* Schmerber v. California, 384 U.S. 757, 765–66 (1966); *Carson*, 296 N.C. at 38, 249 S.E.2d at 422.

c. *See Carson*, 296 N.C. at 38, 249 S.E.2d at 422.

d. *See* State v. Dellinger, 73 N.C. App. 685, 689, 327 S.E.2d 609, 611–12 (1985) (citing State v. Howren, 312 N.C. 454, 323 S.E.2d 335 (1984)).

e. *See* State v. Cain, 79 N.C. App. 35, 43–44, 338 S.E.2d 898, 903–04 (1986); State v. Sadler, 40 N.C. App. 22, 24, 251 S.E.2d 902, 904 (1979) (citing State v. Sanders, 33 N.C. App. 284, 287, 235 S.E.2d 94, 96 (1977)).

f. *See* State v. Leggett, 305 N.C. 213, 219, 287 S.E.2d 832, 836 (1982); State v. Byrd, 78 N.C. App. 627, 628, 337 S.E.2d 665, 666 (1985); State v. Gilliam, 71 N.C. App. 83, 85, 321 S.E.2d 553, 555 (1984).

g. *See* State v. Rollins, 16 N.C. App. 616, 618, 192 S.E.2d 606, 607 (1972) (officers took witness to a poolroom to see if he recognized anyone); State v. Reaves, 15 N.C. App. 476, 478, 190 S.E.2d 358, 360 (1972) (witness identified defendant when he and other prisoners entered a prison box to be tried for various unrelated offenses).

h. *See* State v. Miller, 288 N.C. 582, 590, 220 S.E.2d 326, 333 (1975); State v. Tuggle, 284 N.C. 515, 519, 201 S.E.2d 884, 887 (1974).

i. *See* State v. Coplen, 138 N.C. App. 48, 57, 530 S.E.2d 313, 320 (2000) (citing State v. Odom, 303 N.C. 163, 167, 277 S.E.2d 352, 355 (1981), *cert. denied*, 352 N.C. 677, 545 S.E.2d 438 (2000)).

j. *See* State v. Davis, 349 N.C. 1, 19–20, 506 S.E.2d 455, 465 (1998).

k. *See* Gerstein v. Pugh, 420 U.S. 103, 122 (1975) ("Because of its limited function and its nonadversary character, the probable cause determination is not a 'critical stage' in the prosecution that would require appointed counsel."). A probable cause *hearing* is a critical stage. *See supra* Table 1, note c, at p. 11, and accompanying text.

l. *See* State v. Detter, 298 N.C. 604, 624, 260 S.E.2d 567, 582 (1979) ("It is apparent from the relevant case law that the [first] appearance before a district court judge is not a critical stage because it is not an adversarial judicial proceeding where rights and defenses are preserved or lost or a plea taken."); State v. Gibbs, 335 N.C. 1, 43, 436 S.E.2d 321, 345 (1993) (same).

G.S. 15A-601(a) states that first appearance before a district court judge is not a critical stage in the proceedings. If, as a matter of constitutional law, a court found that a first appearance was in fact a critical stage, the legislature's statement to the contrary would have no effect.

m. *See* State v. Rich, 346 N.C. 50, 55–56, 484 S.E.2d 394, 398 (1997) (noting that prior to the judge's ruling, the issue had been raised twice, attorneys for both sides had been heard twice in separate pretrial hearings, and the proceeding during which the judge announced his ruling was not a hearing).

The United States Supreme Court also has held that a defendant's Sixth Amendment right to the assistance of counsel is abridged when the defendant is not given opportunity to consult with counsel before submitting to a pretrial psychiatric examination.[61] Although the Court did not rule on whether a defendant has a constitutional right to have counsel present during such an examination,[62] the North Carolina Court of Appeals has stated that "[t]here is no constitutional requirement that counsel be present during a psychiatric examination to determine sanity."[63]

Table 2 lists proceedings that the United States Supreme Court and the North Carolina courts have held not to be critical pretrial stages.

[c] Post-Conviction

Defendants have a constitutional right to counsel for first appeals of right.[64] That right includes the right to effective assistance.[65] However, the United States Supreme Court has rejected arguments that defendants have a constitutionally protected right to counsel for discretionary appeals to state appellate courts, *certiorari* petitions to the United States Supreme Court,[66] or post-conviction proceedings, such as motions for appropriate relief.[67]

[3] Covered Offenses
[a] Felonies and Misdemeanors That Result in a Sentence of Imprisonment

The United States Supreme Court has indicated that the Sixth Amendment right to counsel applies to all felony prosecutions.[68] Whether the right applies to misdemeanors depends on whether imprisonment—either an active term or a suspended sentence—is imposed.

---

61. *See* Estelle v. Smith, 451 U.S. 454, 469–71 (1981).

62. *See id.* at 470 n.14.

63. *See* State v. Jackson, 77 N.C. App. 491, 500, 335 S.E.2d 903, 909 (1985), *called into doubt on other grounds*, State v. Huff, 325 N.C. 1, 381 S.E.2d 635 (1989), *vacated on other grounds*, 497 U.S. 1021 (1990).

64. *See* Evitts v. Lucey, 469 U.S. 387 (1985) (grounding such a right in due process); *supra* note 2 (noting right to counsel on first appeal of right).

65. *See Evitts*, 469 U.S. at 396.

66. *See* Wainwright v. Torna, 455 U.S. 586, 587–88 (1982) (no constitutional right to counsel to pursue discretionary state appeal); Ross v. Moffitt, 417 U.S. 600, 610–11 (1974) (no constitutional right to counsel for discretionary state appeals or for *certiorari* petitions to United States Supreme Court).

67. *See* Pennsylvania v. Finely, 481 U.S. 551, 555 (1987) ("We have never held that prisoners have a constitutional right to counsel when mounting collateral attacks upon their convictions and we decline to so hold today.") (citations omitted).

Of course, in North Carolina, criminal defendants have statutory right to counsel in certain post-conviction proceedings. *See* G.S. 7A-451(a)(3).

For a discussion of the cases rejecting the argument that constitutional due process creates a right to counsel in these circumstances, *see* LaFave, *supra* note 2, § 11.1(b).

68. *See* Alabama v. Shelton, 122 S. Ct. 1764 (2002) (citing *Nichols v. United States*,

In *Argersinger v. Hamlin*,[69] the United States Supreme Court held that counsel must be appointed in any criminal prosecution—whether classified as a petty offense, misdemeanor, or felony—"that actually leads to imprisonment."[70] In *Scott v. Illinois*,[71] the Court confirmed *Argersinger*. *Scott* held that in nonfelony cases, there is an actual imprisonment standard for the Sixth Amendment right to counsel: If a sentence of imprisonment is actually imposed, the defendant has a right to counsel; if a fine or other punishment is imposed, no such right applies.[72] In *Alabama v. Shelton*,[73] the United States Supreme Court held that the Sixth Amendment right to counsel also applies to a defendant who receives a suspended sentence.[74] Under *Alabama*, both imposition and activation of a suspended sentence imposed on an uncounseled indigent defendant violate the Sixth Amendment.

[b] Uncharged Offenses

In *Texas v. Cobb*,[75] the United States Supreme Court held that the Sixth Amendment is offense specific. This means that even if the right to counsel has attached for a charged offense, it may not apply to a related uncharged offense.

In *Cobb*, a home was burgled and the residents were missing. The defendant confessed to the burglary but denied knowing what happened to the residents. The defendant was subsequently indicted for the burglary and counsel was appointed. Later, the defendant was arrested for the murder of the residents. After receiving *Miranda* warnings and waiving his rights, the defendant confessed to murdering the residents. The defendant subsequently argued that his confession to the murders was obtained in violation of his Sixth Amendment right to counsel.

The United States Supreme Court rejected the defendant's argument, holding that the Sixth Amendment is offense specific. The Court stated that the Sixth Amendment

---

511 U.S. 738, 743 n.9 (1994), for the proposition that "absent waiver, [the] right to appointed counsel in felony cases is absolute" and stating that for felony convictions "the right to counsel is unquestioned"); LaFave, *supra* note 2, § 11.2(a), at 492 n.10 ("absolute right to appointed counsel in all felony cases").

69. 407 U.S. 25 (1972).

70. *Id.* at 37; *see also Alabama*, 122 S. Ct. at 1767 (so characterizing *Argersinger*).

71. 440 U.S. 367, 373–74 (1979).

72. *See Alabama*, 122 S. Ct. at 1767 (so characterizing *Scott*). If an uncounseled misdemeanor conviction is valid under *Scott*, it may be used to enhance punishment for a subsequent conviction. *See id.* at 1770 (discussing holding of *Nichols v. United States*, 511 U.S. 738, 741 (1994)).

73. 122 S. Ct. 1764 (2002).

74. In *State v. Lambert*, 146 N.C. App. 360, 553 S.E.2d 71 (2001), *review denied by* 355 N.C. 289, 561 S.E.2d 271 (2002), the North Carolina Court of Appeals held that the right to counsel does not apply at resentencing when the trial court is not likely to resentence the defendant to an active term of imprisonment. *See supra* p. 7 (discussing *Lambert*). This holding is now questionable in light of *Alabama*.

75. 532 U.S. 162 (2001).

does not apply to uncharged crimes that are merely factually related to the charged offense—as the murders were related to the burglary. The Court held that the Sixth Amendment only applies to uncharged crimes that are the same as the charged one. The test for determining whether offenses are the same is the test set forth in *Blockburger v. United States*[76] for determining whether offenses are the same for purposes of double jeopardy. Under that test, offenses are not the same if each has an element that is not in the other. Applying its holding, the Court held that since murder and burglary were not the same offenses under *Blockburger*, the defendant's Sixth Amendment right to counsel for the murder charge did not attach when he was indicted for the factually related burglary offense. North Carolina cases decided before *Cobb* are consistent with this holding.[77]

The United States Court of Appeals for the Fifth Circuit recently applied *Cobb* to hold that even if the uncharged offense is the same as a charged offense under *Blockburger*, the Sixth Amendment right to counsel does not attach with regard to the uncharged offense if it is being prosecuted by a separate sovereign.[78] Essentially, the Fifth Circuit viewed *Cobb*'s incorporation of the *Blockburger* same elements test into Sixth Amendment analysis as also endorsing incorporation of other aspects of double jeopardy analysis.[79] It is well settled that under the double jeopardy dual sovereignty doctrine, double jeopardy does not apply to prosecutions by separate sovereigns, whether they be the federal government and a state[80] or two states.[81]

§ 1.03 Attorney Error Claims

Once it has been determined that the defendant had a constitutionally protected right to counsel at the time of the alleged ineffectiveness, the claim must be analyzed under the relevant test. In *Strickland v. Washington*,[82] the United States Supreme Court set forth a two-part test for evaluating attorney error IAC claims asserted under the Sixth

---

76. 284 U.S. 299 (1932).

77. *See, e.g.*, State v. Warren, 348 N.C. 80, 95–96, 499 S.E.2d 431, 439 (1998) ("the Sixth Amendment is offense-specific"; going on to note that some jurisdictions have adopted a "very closely related crime" exception but holding that even if the crimes at issue were "inextricably intertwined," the exception still would not apply); State v. Hall, 131 N.C. App. 427, 435, 508 S.E.2d 8, 14 (1998) (Sixth Amendment right to counsel is "offense specific" and "even if a defendant invokes . . . right to counsel in one case, officers may still interrogate him in regard to other offenses") (citing State v. Pope, 333 N.C. 106, 113, 423 S.E.2d 740, 744 (1992), *aff'd*, 350 N.C. 303 (1999)).

78. *See* United States v. Avants, 278 F.3d 510 (5th Cir. 2002), *cert. denied*, 122 S. Ct. 2683 (2002).

79. *See id.* at 517.

80. *See* Abbatte v. United States, 359 U.S. 187 (1959); State v. Myers, 82 N.C. App. 299, 346 S.E.2d 273 (1986).

81. *See* Heath v. Alabama, 474 U.S. 82 (1985).

82. 466 U.S. 668 (1984).

and Fourteenth Amendments. In *State v. Braswell*,[83] the North Carolina Supreme Court adopted the *Strickland* test as the standard for evaluating attorney error IAC claims asserted under the North Carolina Constitution.[84] Attorney error IAC claims are claims in which the defendant alleges that counsel erroneously handled the case by, for example, failing to object to evidence, request proper jury instructions, or file notice of appeal when asked to do so. These claims are distinguishable from those involving fact patterns where, for example, the defendant is denied counsel or counsel labors under a conflict of interest.[85]

Under the two-pronged *Strickland* test, illustrated in Table 3, a defendant asserting attorney error must first show that counsel's performance was "deficient."[86] Under the second prong of the analysis, a defendant must show that the deficient performance prejudiced the defense.[87] If the court can determine at the outset that no prejudice resulted from the alleged ineffectiveness, it need not determine whether counsel's performance was actually deficient. In other words, it is permissible for a court to resolve IAC claims by deciding the second prong of the IAC analysis first.[88] This test applies without modification to a great variety of IAC claims.[89]

83. 312 N.C. 553, 324 S.E.2d 241 (1985).

84. 312 N.C. at 562, 324 S.E.2d at 248 ("we expressly adopt the test set out in *Strickland v. Washington* as a uniform standard to be applied to measure [IAC] under the North Carolina Constitution").

85. For a discussion of the relevant standards to be applied in these contexts, *see infra* pp. 22–33 (denial of counsel); pp. 34–48 (conflict of interest).

86. *Strickland*, 466 U.S. at 687.

87. *See id.*

88. *See id.* at 697; *Braswell*, 312 N.C. at 563, 324 S.E.2d at 249.

89. In *Williams v. Taylor*, 529 U.S. 362 (2000), the United States Supreme Court noted "that while the *Strickland* test provides sufficient guidance for resolving virtually all [IAC] claims, there are situations in which the overriding focus on fundamental fairness may affect the analysis." *Id.* at 391. Thus, the Court explained, there are situations where prejudice may be presumed. Such situations include those that involve a denial of counsel or conflict of interest. *See id.* (citing that portion of the *Strickland* opinion that identifies these situations as warranting a presumption of prejudice); *see infra* pp. 22–48 (discussing denial of counsel and conflict of interest cases). The *Williams* Court continued, noting another category of claims in which the focus on fundamental fairness affects the analysis: those claims in which "it would be unjust to characterize the likelihood of a different outcome as legitimate 'prejudice.'" *See Williams*, 529 U.S. at 391–92. The Court explained: "Even if a defendant's false testimony might have persuaded the jury to acquit him, it is not fundamentally unfair to conclude that he was not prejudiced by counsel's interference with his intended perjury." *See id.* at 392 (citing *Nix v. Whiteside*, 475 U.S. 157 (1986), and offering the facts of *Lockhart v. Fretwell*, 506 U.S. 364 (1993), as another example of a case in this category). Focusing on this second category of claims, the Court clarified that the common feature among the claims is that they involve situations where the defendant is not deprived of a substantive or procedural right to which he or she is entitled. *See id.* at 393. When such a deprivation does occur, however, these cases "do not justify a departure from a straightforward application of *Strickland*." *Id.*

Table 3: Two-Pronged *Strickland* Test

1. Deficient performance
2. Prejudice

---

[1] Deficient Performance

The first prong of the *Strickland* test—deficient performance—requires a showing that counsel's performance fell below an objective standard of reasonableness.[90] The Constitution does not guarantee flawless performance; it guarantees only objectively reasonable performance.[91] Objectively reasonable performance is performance that is reasonable under prevailing professional norms[92] and "make[s] the adversarial testing process work in the particular case."[93] The United States Supreme Court has recognized that no set of rules "can satisfactorily take account of the variety of circumstances faced by defense counsel or the range of legitimate decisions regarding how best to represent a criminal defendant."[94] Thus, the deciding court must evaluate the reasonableness of defense counsel's conduct on a case-by-case basis and must consider all of the circumstances. The Court has expressly rejected the adoption of per se rules regarding deficient performance.[95]

Additionally, when judging reasonableness, the court must not engage in hindsight; rather, it must consider counsel's conduct as of the time of the alleged deficient performance.[96] "Because of the difficulties inherent in making the evaluation, a court must

---

90. *Strickland*, 466 U.S. at 687–88.

91. *See* United States v. Cronic, 466 U.S. 648, 656 (1984) (recognizing that the fact that counsel may have made demonstrable errors does not necessarily mean counsel was ineffective).

92. *See Strickland*, 466 U.S. at 688. Prevailing norms of practice are guides to determining what is reasonable, not rules for such a determination. *See id.* Strickland indicated that prevailing norms of practice can be found in "American Bar Association standards and the like." *Id. See generally* ABA STANDARDS FOR CRIMINAL JUSTICE: PROSECUTION FUNCTION AND DEFENSE FUNCTION (1993) (setting forth standards for the defense function).

93. *Strickland*, 466 U.S. at 690.

94. *Id.* at 689–90; *see also* Roe v. Flores-Ortega, 528 U.S. 470, 477 (2000) (quoting same).

95. *See Roe*, 528 U.S. at 478 (rejecting a per se rule requiring counsel to either file a notice of appeal or discuss the possibility of an appeal with the defendant, ascertain his wishes, and act accordingly; explaining that a per se rule would be "inconsistent with *Strickland*'s holding that 'the performance inquiry must be whether counsel's assistance was reasonable considering all the circumstances'") (quoting *Strickland*, 466 U.S. at 688).

96. *See Strickland*, 466 U.S. at 689 ("A fair assessment of attorney performance requires that every effort be made to eliminate the distorting effects of hindsight, to reconstruct the circumstances of counsel's challenged conduct, and to evaluate the conduct from counsel's perspective at the time."); *Roe*, 528 U.S. at 477 ("courts must 'judge the reasonableness of counsel's conduct on the facts of the particular case, viewed as of the time of counsel's conduct'") (quoting *Strickland*, 466 U.S. at 690); *see also* State v. Mason, 337 N.C. 165, 177–78, 446 S.E.2d 58, 65 (1994) (quoting *Strickland*).

indulge a strong presumption that counsel's conduct falls within the wide range of reasonable professional assistance."[97]

When analyzing claims under this prong of the *Strickland* test, courts occasionally label counsel's decision or action "strategic" or "tactical" and then indicate that they will not second-guess such a decision. Such a view renders any strategic or tactical decision unassailable. However, such a view is at odds with the language of the *Strickland* decision. While *Strickland* recognized that "strategic choices made after thorough investigation of law and facts relevant to plausible options are virtually unchallengeable,"[98] it also recognized that strategic choices made after "less than complete investigation" are reasonable only "to the extent that reasonable professional judgments support the limitations on investigation."[99] Thus, when a strategic or tactical decision is challenged, the court must determine whether the decision was made after thorough investigation of the relevant law and facts. If so, the decision is, in the words of *Strickland*, "virtually unchallengeable." If not, the court must inquire whether the limitation on investigation was reasonable. Of course, the defendant bears the burden of rebutting the presumption that counsel's conduct was reasonable.[100]

[2] Prejudice

Under the second prong of the *Strickland* test, the defendant must show that the deficient performance prejudiced the defense.[101] When an IAC claim is raised after a jury trial, this requires the defendant to show that "counsel's errors were so serious as to deprive the defendant of a fair trial, a trial whose result is reliable."[102] This means that an error does not warrant reversal of a conviction unless there is a "reasonable probability that, but for counsel's . . . errors, the result of the proceeding would have been different."[103] A reasonable probability "is a probability sufficient to undermine confidence in the outcome."[104] When a defendant challenges a conviction, the inquiry focuses on whether "there is a reasonable probability that absent the errors, the factfinder would

---

97. *Strickland*, 466 U.S. at 689; *see also Roe*, 528 U.S. at 477; *Mason*, 337 N.C. at 177–78, 446 S.E.2d at 65 (same).

98. *Strickland*, 466 U.S. at 690.

99. *Id.* at 690–91.

100. *See supra* p. 17 (discussing the standard for determining whether counsel's conduct was reasonable).

101. *See Strickland*, 466 U.S. at 687, 692.

102. *Id.* at 687.

103. *Id.* at 694; *see also* State v. Braswell, 312 N.C. 553, 563, 324 S.E.2d 241, 249 (1985).

104. *Strickland*, 466 U.S. at 694.
This standard of prejudice derives from the test for materiality of exculpatory information not disclosed to the defense by the prosecution and from the test for materiality of testimony made unavailable to the defense by government deportation of a witness. *See id.* at 694. In adopting this test, the Supreme Court expressly rejected a stricter outcome-determinative standard that would have required the defendant to show that counsel's deficient conduct more likely than not altered the outcome in the case. *See id.* at 693–94.

have had a reasonable doubt respecting guilt."[105] If the challenge is to a death sentence, the inquiry focuses on "whether there is a reasonable probability that, absent the errors, the sentencer . . . would have concluded that the balance of aggravating and mitigating circumstances did not warrant death."[106] And finally, when an IAC claim is raised after a guilty plea, the inquiry focuses on whether "there is a reasonable probability that, but for counsel's errors, [the defendant] would not have pleaded guilty and would have insisted on going to trial."[107] If the IAC challenge is to a guilty plea, the defendant must allege that but for counsel's deficient performance, he or she would not have pleaded guilty.[108]

In making the determination regarding prejudice, it is appropriate to consider the weight of the evidence. A verdict supported by overwhelming evidence is less likely to have been affected by deficient performance than a verdict supported by weak or conflicting evidence.[109]

In 2001, the United States Supreme Court decided *Glover v. United States*.[110] In *Glover*, the Court found the facts sufficient to warrant a finding of prejudice under the second prong of the *Strickland* test. The case involved defense counsel's failure to press for grouping of the defendant's convictions for purposes of sentencing under applicable federal law. The trial court decided not to group the offenses, which resulted in a sentence six to twenty-one months greater than the sentence would have been if the offenses had been grouped. The federal trial court rejected the defendant's IAC claim, holding that the six to twenty-one month increase in sentence was not significant enough to amount to prejudice. The United States Court of Appeals for the Seventh Circuit agreed. The Supreme Court reversed, holding that its prior decisions "do not suggest that a minimal amount of additional time in prison cannot

---

105. *Strickland*, 466 U.S. at 695.

106. *Id.*

107. *See* Hill v. Lockhart, 474 U.S. 52, 59 (1985); *see also* State v. Ager, 152 N.C. App. 577, 568 S.E.2d 328 (2002) (citing *Hill* for this proposition). In *Hill*, the United States Supreme court explained that in many guilty plea cases, analysis of the second prong of the *Strickland* test will "closely resemble" analysis of that prong in cases that go to trial. *Hill*, 474 U.S. at 59. It stated:

> For example, where the alleged error of counsel is a failure to investigate or discover potentially exculpatory evidence, the determination whether the error "prejudiced" the defendant by causing him to plead guilty rather than go to trial will depend on the likelihood that discovery of the evidence would have led counsel to change his recommendation as to the plea. This assessment, in turn, will depend in large part on a prediction whether the evidence likely would have changed the outcome of a trial. Similarly, where the alleged error of counsel is a failure to advise the defendant of a potential affirmative defense to the crime charged, the resolution of the "prejudice" inquiry will depend largely on whether the affirmative defense likely would have succeeded at trial.

Id.

108. *See id.*

109. *See Strickland*, 466 U.S. at 696.

110. 531 U.S. 198 (2001).

constitute prejudice."[111] The Court concluded that in the case before it, "it is clear that prejudice flowed from the asserted error in sentencing."[112]

In certain circumstances, a defendant is relieved of the burden of showing actual prejudice under the second prong of the *Strickland* analysis and prejudice is presumed. In *Roe v. Flores-Ortega*,[113] the United States Supreme Court explained that it normally applies a strong presumption of reliability of judicial proceedings and requires a defendant to overcome that presumption.[114] Thus, "in cases involving mere 'attorney error,' we require the defendant to demonstrate that the errors 'actually had an adverse effect on the defense.'"[115] The Court distinguished "attorney error" cases, where the defendant alleges that counsel made specific errors in the course of representation, from cases in which the defendant alleges that during the judicial proceeding he or she was denied the assistance of counsel. As to the latter category of cases, the Court stated: "The presumption that counsel's assistance is essential requires us to conclude that a trial is unfair if the accused is denied counsel at a critical stage. The same is true on appeal. Under such circumstances, no specific showing of prejudice is required, because the adversary process itself is presumptively unreliable."[116] The Court went on to extend this presumption of prejudice rule to include situations where attorney ineffectiveness results in a proceeding not occurring at all.[117]

In *Roe*, the defendant alleged that counsel was ineffective by failing to file a notice of appeal, even though the defendant had not clearly conveyed his desire to appeal to counsel. Vacating and remanding, the Court began by setting out the standard for determining whether counsel's performance in connection with the appeal was deficient under the first prong of *Strickland*.[118] Moving on to the standard to be applied under *Strickland*'s prejudice prong, the Court held that when counsel's deficient per-

---

111. *Id.* at 203.

112. *Id.* at 204.

113. 528 U.S. 470 (2000).

114. *See id.* at 482.

115. *Id.* (quoting *Strickland*, 466 U.S. at 693).

116. *Id.* at 483 (quotations and citations omitted); *see infra* pp. 22–33 (discussing denial of counsel cases).

117. *See Roe*, 528 U.S. at 484. ("[we] presum[e] prejudice with no further showing from the defendant of the merits of his underlying claims when the violation of the right to counsel rendered the proceeding presumptively unreliable or entirely nonexistent").

118. The Court held:
> [C]ounsel has a constitutionally-imposed duty to consult with the defendant about an appeal when there is reason to think either (1) that a rational defendant would want to appeal (for example, because there are nonfrivolous grounds for appeal), or (2) that this particular defendant reasonably demonstrated to counsel that he was interested in appealing.

528 U.S. at 480. Ultimately, the Court remanded for further proceedings consistent with its opinion. *See id.* at 487.

formance actually deprives a defendant of an appeal that he or she would have otherwise taken, prejudice will be presumed.[119] It reasoned: "Put simply, we cannot accord any presumption of reliability to judicial proceedings that never took place."[120] The Court was careful to point out that the presumption of prejudice did not mean that a defendant is entitled to relief solely on a showing that counsel performed deficiently with respect to the appeal. The Court clarified that a critical component of any such claim is proof that counsel's deficient performance "actually cause[d] the forfeiture of the defendant's appeal."[121] It held that, in these circumstances, a defendant must show that there is a reasonable probability that but for counsel's deficient conduct, he or she would have timely appealed.[122] Thus, under *Roe*, prejudice will be presumed when counsel's deficient performance leads to the forfeiture of a legal proceeding. Denial of counsel cases—which *Roe* recognized also warrant a presumption of prejudice—are discussed in the section that follows.[123]

---

119. *See id.* at 483 ("[t]he . . . denial of the entire judicial proceeding itself, which a defendant wanted at the time and to which he had a right, . . . demands a presumption of prejudice").

120. *Id.* at 483 (quotation and citation omitted).

121. *Id.* at 484.

122. *See id.*

123. One issue that may arise for the trial judge in connection with attorney error ineffectiveness is what to do when the trial judge suspects ineffectiveness in the course of trial. If counsel is in fact ineffective and defendant makes a motion to remove or replace the lawyer, such a motion should be granted. *See generally infra* § 2.01[19] (listing cases involving withdrawal or discharge of counsel). The more difficult situation arises where the defendant makes no such motion but the court suspects ineffectiveness. *State v. Nelson*, 76 N.C. App. 371, 372–74, 333 S.E.2d 499, 500–02 (1985), *modified and aff'd*, 316 N.C. 350, 341 S.E.2d 561 (1986), may suggest an answer. In *Nelson*, attorney Fitch was appointed to represent an indigent defendant. Several months before trial, the defendant's relatives hired attorney Farris to assist Fitch. On the day of trial, Fitch had a family medical emergency and was unable to appear in court. When the judge learned of this, he refused to continue the case and *ex mero motu* entered an order permitting Fitch to withdraw. Farris then made a motion to withdraw because, among other reasons, the defendant did not want him for a lawyer. The trial judge denied this motion. On appeal, defendant argued that by discharging his court-appointed lawyer, the trial court deprived him of his right to effective assistance of counsel. The North Carolina Court of Appeals agreed. It began by stating that once counsel is appointed to represent an indigent defendant, the appointment of substitute counsel is constitutionally required "only when it appears that representation by original counsel could deprive defendant of his right to effective assistance of counsel." It continued, holding that "when an indigent defendant has confidence in and is satisfied with the appointed lawyer that has handled the case . . . he should not be deprived of that counsel's services during the trial except for justifiable cause." In the case before it, the court found no justifiable cause.

Thus, *Nelson* implies that even if the defendant is satisfied with counsel, removal is appropriate where there is justifiable cause. Ineffectiveness surely is such a cause. However, because a claim of ineffectiveness must rebut the presumption of reasonable professional

§ 1.04 Denial of Counsel Claims

Defendants do not always frame their IAC claims as involving attorney error that prejudiced the defense. Sometimes, defendants assert that a denial of counsel resulted in a violation of their Sixth Amendment right to effective assistance of counsel. Denial of counsel cases are analyzed under a standard set forth in *Strickland*'s companion case, *United States v. Cronic*.[124]

In *Cronic*, the defendant was indicted on federal mail fraud charges. When the defendant's counsel withdrew shortly before trial, the district court appointed a young real estate lawyer to represent him. The trial court allowed the lawyer only twenty-five days to prepare for trial, even though it had taken the government four and a half years to investigate the case and review thousands of documents. The defendant was convicted and sentenced to twenty-five years' imprisonment. The defendant appealed, asserting a violation of his Sixth Amendment right to effective assistance of counsel. In due course, the case came before the United States Supreme Court.

Holding that no Sixth Amendment violation had occurred, the Court set forth the standard that applies in denial of counsel cases. The *Cronic* Court noted that certain circumstances "are so likely to prejudice the accused that the cost of litigating their effect in a particular case is unjustified."[125] It identified such circumstances as including those in which there is an actual or constructive denial of counsel.[126] Thus, to successfully assert a *Cronic* claim, a defendant only need show a denial of counsel—actual or constructive—that rises to the level of a violation of Sixth Amendment rights. No prejudice need be shown.[127] The various types of claims that are covered by the *Cronic* rule are illustrated in Table 4.

---

assistance, *see supra* p. 18, ineffectiveness rarely can be established on the face of the trial record. Thus, where defendant does not wish to discharge counsel, it appears unlikely that, absent ineffectiveness per se, *see infra* § 1.06 (*Harbison* claims), the court will have the necessary facts to find that counsel has been ineffective. If, in an abundance of caution, the trial judge decides to discharge counsel and appoint a substitute over the defendant's objection, the defendant may later claim, as in *Nelson*, that absent proof of ineffectiveness, the trial court's order deprived him or her of the right to counsel.

124. 466 U.S. 648 (1984).

125. *Id.* at 658.

126. The *Cronic* Court also noted that counsel conflict of interest claims present circumstances where the likelihood of prejudice is so high that it need not be litigated. *See id.* at 662 n.31 ("we have presumed prejudice when counsel labors under an actual conflict of interest"). Such claims are discussed *infra* pp. 34–48.

127. *See Cronic*, 466 U.S. at 659–62; Roe v. Flores-Ortega, 528 U.S. 470, 483 (2000) (discussing *Cronic* rule); Mickens v. Taylor, 122 S. Ct. 1237 (2002) ("We have spared the defendant the need of showing probable effect upon the outcome, and have simply presumed such effect, where assistance of counsel has been denied entirely or during a critical stage of the proceeding.").

Table 4: Types of Denial of Counsel Claims

Actual Denial of Counsel	Constructive Denial of Counsel
No lawyer at all	Total failure to subject the State's case to meaningful adversarial testing
No lawyer at a critical stage	No lawyer could provide effective assistance

---

[1]   Actual Denial of Counsel

Turning to a discussion of the circumstances that fall within its rule—that is, those circumstances so likely to cause prejudice that the cost of litigating their effect is unjustified and a presumption of prejudice is required—the *Cronic* Court noted first and "[m]ost obvious" the actual denial of counsel.[128] The Court reasoned that the presumption that counsel's assistance is essential required it to conclude that a trial is unfair if the accused is denied counsel at a critical stage of his or her trial.[129]

At the extreme, actual denial of counsel cases involve fact patterns where the defendant has no lawyer at all. *Penson v. Ohio*[130] is an example. In *Penson*, an indigent defendant was appointed counsel for his state appeal. Subsequently, and without following the procedures set out in *Anders v. California*,[131] the state appellate court granted appointed counsel's motion to withdraw. After finding that the record supported several arguably meritorious grounds for reversal of the defendant's conviction and modification of his sentence, the state appellate court considered the merits of the defendant's appeal without appointing new counsel. The United States Supreme Court held that the denial of counsel left the defendant "completely without representation during the appellate court's actual decisional process."[132] In such a scenario, the Court concluded, prejudice must be presumed.[133]

Penson illustrates an actual denial of counsel case covered by the *Cronic* rule. However, the *Cronic* Court expressly recognized that its rule applies not only to cases where the defendant was completely without counsel but also to cases where the defendant had counsel but counsel was somehow prevented from assisting the defendant during a critical stage of the proceedings.[134] The Court went on to cite several prior cases illustrating this latter category, including *Geders v. United States*.[135] In *Geders*, the defendant

---

128. *Cronic*, 466 U.S. at 659; *see also* Bell v. Cone, 122 S. Ct. 1843 (2002).

129. *See Cronic*, 466 U.S. at 659.

130. 488 U.S. 75 (1988).

131. 386 U.S. 738 (1967).

132. *Penson*, 488 U.S. at 88.

133. *See id.* at 88–89.

134. *See Cronic*, 466 U.S. at 659 n.25 ("The court has uniformly found constitutional error without any showing of prejudice when counsel was either totally absent, or prevented from assisting the accused during a critical stage of the proceeding."); *see also* Mickens v. Taylor, 122 S. Ct. 1237 (2002) (presumption of prejudice applies "where assistance of counsel has been denied entirely or during a critical stage of the proceeding").

135. 425 U.S. 80 (1976); *see also* Bell v. Cone, 122 S. Ct. 1843 n.3 (2002). For a discussion of the meaning of the term "critical stage," see *supra* p. 5.

was not denied counsel altogether. Rather, the trial court issued an order directing the defendant not to consult with counsel during a seventeen-hour overnight recess called while the defendant was on the stand for direct examination, and shortly before cross-examination. The United States Supreme Court held that the trial court's order violated the defendant's Sixth Amendment right to the assistance of counsel.[136] No showing of prejudice was required.

The *Cronic* Court cited other partial denial of counsel cases where a presumption of prejudice had been applied. Among them were cases where state law empowered judges in criminal nonjury cases to deny defense counsel any opportunity to make closing arguments;[137] where state law restricted defense counsel's right to decide whether and when the defendant should take the stand;[138] where the defendant was denied counsel at arraignment[139] or at a preliminary hearing;[140] and where state law, while allowing defendants to testify through unsworn statements, prevented defense counsel from eliciting the defendants' testimony through direct examination.[141]

Although the North Carolina Supreme Court's decision in *State v. Colbert*[142] does not mention *Cronic*, it is consistent with the ruling in that case. In *Colbert*, defense counsel was not present when the defendant's case was called for trial. Notwithstanding the absence of counsel, the trial court allowed jury selection to proceed. After being convicted, the defendant appealed, asserting that he was denied his right to counsel.

---

136. *See Geders*, 425 U.S. at 91. The Court explained:

> It is common practice during [overnight] recesses for an accused and counsel to discuss the events of the day's trial. Such recesses are often times of intensive work, with tactical decisions to be made and strategies to be reviewed. The lawyer may need to obtain from his client information made relevant by the day's testimony, or he may need to pursue inquiry along lines not fully explored earlier. At the least, the overnight recess during trial gives the defendant a chance to discuss with counsel the significance of the day's events.

Id. at 88.

137. *See* Herring v. New York, 422 U.S. 853 (1975). The *Herring* Court expressly recognized that its holding did not mean that closing arguments in a criminal case "must be uncontrolled or even unrestrained." *Id.* at 862. The Court recognized that the presiding judge must be given "great latitude" in controlling the duration and limiting the scope of closing arguments. *Id.*

138. *See* Brooks v. Tennessee, 406 U.S. 605, 612–13 (1972). The *Brooks* Court noted that its holding should not be read to "curtail[] in any way the ordinary power of a trial judge to set the order of proof." *Id.* at 613.

139. *See* Hamilton v. Alabama, 368 U.S. 52, 54–55 (1961) ("When one pleads to a capital charge without benefit of counsel, we do not stop to determine whether prejudice resulted.").

140. *See* White v. Maryland, 373 U.S. 59, 60 (1963) ("We repeat what we said in [*Hamilton*], that we do not stop to determine whether prejudice resulted.").

141. *See* Ferguson v. Georgia, 365 U.S. 570 (1961).

142. 311 N.C. 283, 316 S.E.2d 79 (1984).

Noting that jury selection is a critical stage of a criminal trial, the court agreed and ordered a new trial.[143]

Subsequently, the North Carolina Supreme Court expressly relied on *Colbert* and *Cronic* to require a new trial in an actual denial of counsel case. In *State v. Luker*,[144] after the State rested, the defendant and his counsel disagreed over whether the defendant should testify. Counsel believed that the defendant's testimony would prejudice the defense; the defendant insisted that he wished to take the stand. Counsel stated that he would withdraw if the defendant testified. The defendant chose to testify, and counsel was discharged by the court. On appeal, the defendant argued that by forcing him to choose between being represented by counsel and taking the stand in his own defense, his right to counsel was violated. The North Carolina Court of Appeals held that although the defendant was denied his right to assistance of counsel, the error was harmless. The North Carolina Supreme Court agreed that the defendant was denied his Sixth Amendment right to counsel but, citing *Colbert* and *Cronic*, held that the court of appeals had erred in concluding that the denial did not require reversal.

[2] Constructive Denial of Counsel

The second set of circumstances covered by the *Cronic* rule involves constructive denials of counsel. Specifically, the *Cronic* Court identified circumstances where "counsel entirely fails to subject the prosecution's case to meaningful adversarial testing" and where "the likelihood that any lawyer, even a fully competent one, could provide effective assistance is . . . small."[145] This book refers to these circumstances as constructive denial of counsel cases.

[a]   Total Failure to Subject the State's Case to Meaningful Adversarial Testing

As indicated above, *Cronic* included within its rule cases where counsel "entirely fails to subject the prosecution's case to meaningful adversarial testing."[146] The Court was careful to note that unless such a deprivation—a total failure to subject the State's case to meaningful adversarial testing—occurs, the case should be viewed as one involving

---

143. The *Colbert* court explained:

> It is essential that counsel be present during the entire jury voir dire so that he may intelligently exercise defendant's right to peremptory challenges. . . .
>
> . . .
>
> Here, defendant's counsel did not observe any of the state's questioning of the jurors. Of course, defendant's counsel could, and perhaps did, excuse one or more of the jurors passed by the state. But in so doing he was acting at least partially in the dark as he knew nothing of what had transpired in his absence. This does not comport with the right to counsel. . . .

311 N.C. at 285–86, 316 S.E.2d at 80–81.

144. 311 N.C. 301, 316 S.E.2d 309 (1984).

145. United States v. Cronic, 466 U.S. 648, 659–60 (1984); *see also* Bell v. Cone, 122 S. Ct. 1843 (2002).

146. *Cronic*, 466 U.S. at 659.

mere attorney error to which the *Strickland* test applies.[147] *Cronic*, however, did not provide a bright-line rule for determining when a case involves only attorney error and thus is subject to *Strickland* or when it involves a failure to subject the State's case to meaningful adversarial testing and thus is within the scope of *Cronic*. That job was left to the lower courts.

The lower courts have struggled for clarity on this issue, repeatedly trying to articulate where the relevant line should be drawn between *Cronic* and *Strickland*.[148] The First Circuit put it like this: Claims alleging "maladroit performance" are analyzed under *Strickland*; claims alleging "non-performance" are analyzed under *Cronic*.[149] The Fifth Circuit stated that "when the defendant can establish that counsel was not merely incompetent but inert," *Cronic* will apply.[150] That court identified the critical question as "whether the [defendant] asserts that he received incompetent counsel or none at all."[151] The Ninth Circuit held that *Cronic* applies when counsel committed "not merely a negligent misstep in an attempt to champion his client's cause . . . [but] an abandonment of the defense of his client at a critical stage."[152]

In the end, these general statements may not be very helpful. Even courts that agree on the general statements do not always agree on how they apply to a particular set of facts.[153] Thus, a review of the actual cases is necessary. Although there do not appear to be any published North Carolina appellate cases on point, relevant federal circuit court cases can be found. A review of the federal decisions reveals that the federal courts tend to apply this line of constructive denial analysis (the total failure to subject the State's case to a meaningful adversarial testing line) in two categories of cases: complete failure to act cases and prosecutor's aide cases.

[i]   Complete Failure to Act Cases

In complete failure to act cases, counsel fails to provide any meaningful assistance

---

147. *See id.* at 659 n.26 ("Apart from circumstances of that magnitude, however, there is generally no basis for finding a Sixth Amendment violation unless the accused can show how specific errors of counsel undermined the reliability of the finding of guilt."); *see generally supra* pp. 15–21 (discussing the *Strickland* test).

148. The difficulty in drawing this line is well illustrated by the United States Supreme Court's recent decision in *Bell v. Cone*, 122 S. Ct. 1843 (2002). In that case, the state courts applied *Strickland*, the Sixth Circuit applied *Cronic*, and the Supreme Court reversed, holding that the state court was right and *Strickland* applied.

149. Scarpa v. Dubois, 38 F.3d 1, 15 (1st Cir. 1994).

150. Childress v. Johnson, 103 F.3d 1221, 1228 (5th Cir. 1997).

151. *Id.* at 1230.

152. United States v. Swanson, 943 F.2d 1070, 1074 (9th Cir. 1991).

153. *See, e.g., Childress*, 103 F.3d at 1229 n.12 ("While gleaning insight from *Swanson*'s statement of Sixth Amendment principles, we do not necessarily endorse its finding of a constructive denial of counsel. Defense counsel in *Swanson* failed to call witnesses and conceded in his closing argument that the evidence of his client's guilt was overwhelming. These appear to be trial errors amenable to *Strickland* analysis.").

during a critical stage of the proceeding. The federal circuit courts have found a constructive denial of counsel where

- counsel, appointed for only a ten-day period during which a competency hearing was held, failed to conduct any investigation into the defendant's competency;[154]
- counsel offered no assistance to the defendant at plea proceedings;[155]
- counsel refused to participate in the defendant's trial;[156]
- counsel made no attempt to represent the defendant's interests and acted as a "mere spectator" at the defendant's resentencing;[157] and
- counsel was silent throughout "virtually the entire trial," including "most crucially" when the judge directed a verdict against the defendant.[158]

Similarly, the United States Court of Appeals for the Fourth Circuit has opined that where counsel sleeps through significant portions of a critical stage of the proceedings, defendant is constructively denied counsel.[159]

---

154. *See* Appel v. Horn, 250 F.3d 203, 217 (3rd Cir. 2001).

155. *See* Childress, 103 F.3d at 1231 ("[W]e are convinced that counsel, though surely more sentient than a potted plant, was not the advocate for the defense whose assistance is contemplated by the Sixth Amendment.").

156. *See* Martin v. Rose, 744 F.2d 1245, 1250–51 (6th Cir. 1984).

157. Tucker v. Day, 969 F.2d 155, 159 (5th Cir.1992).

158. Harding v. Davis, 878 F.2d 1341, 1345 (11th Cir.1989).

159. *See* Glover v. Miro, 262 F.3d 268, 277 (4th Cir. 2001) (distinguishing the case before it from "one where the lawyer literally sleeps through the State's case or otherwise might as well be absent from the proceedings"), *cert. denied*, 122 S. Ct. 1966 (2002). The Fifth Circuit's view is that "[u]nconscious counsel equates to no counsel at all" and is an actual rather than a constructive denial of counsel. *See* Burdine v. Johnson, 262 F.3d 336, 349 (5th Cir. 2001) (holding that defendant was denied effective assistance warranting a presumption of prejudice when counsel repeatedly slept during the guilt–innocence phase of his capital trial), *cert. denied*, 122 S. Ct. 2347 (2002). The Fifth Circuit distinguished sleeping counsel from counsel functioning under the influence of alcohol or drugs, stating:
> Even the intoxicated attorney exercises judgment, though perhaps impaired, on behalf of his client at all times during a trial. Yet, the attorney that is unconscious during critical stages of a trial is simply not capable of exercising judgment. The unconscious attorney is in fact not different from an attorney that is physically absent from trial since both are equally unable to exercise judgment on behalf of their clients.

Id. at 349.

The disagreement between the circuits regarding whether to characterize sleeping counsel cases as actual or constructive denial of counsel cases has no practical import; regardless of the characterization, both circuits agree that the *Cronic* rule applies.

Recognizing that the *Cronic* constructive denial exception is very narrow,[160] the courts have been careful to distinguish complete failure to act cases from those in which counsel offered some meaningful assistance but failed to act on a particular issue or issues.[161] The United States Supreme Court, in *Bell v. Cone*,[162] recently approved of this distinction.

In *Bell*, a capital defendant claimed that his counsel was ineffective during the sentencing phase by failing to present mitigating evidence and by waiving final argument. The defendant further argued that because his counsel failed to "mount some case for life" after the State introduced evidence at sentencing and gave a closing argument, *Cronic*, not *Strickland*, applied. The Court disagreed, stating that when *Cronic* addressed counsel's failure to act, it indicated that the failure "must be complete" and "entire[]." The Court continued:

> Here, respondent's argument is not that his counsel failed to oppose the prosecution throughout the sentencing proceedings as a whole, but that his counsel failed to do so at specific points. For purposes of distinguishing the rule of *Strickland* and that of *Cronic*, this difference is not of degree but of kind.[163]

---

160. *See* McGurk v. Stenberg, 163 F.3d 470, 473 (8th Cir. 1998) (recognizing "the extremely limited circumstances in which it is appropriate to presume prejudice" and noting that "courts have been appropriately cautious in presuming prejudice); *Glover*, 262 F.3d at 277 ("In fact, it will be the rare claim of ineffective assistance that is tantamount to a constructive denial of counsel. *Strickland* remains the norm for ineffective assistance claims, and the Supreme Court has made clear that it will not countenance a per-se prejudice exception which will swallow the actual prejudice *Strickland* rule.").

161. *See Glover*, 262 F.3d at 276 (holding that defendant was not constructively denied counsel where counsel "acted as [defendant's] advocate at every step," including: contacting some potential witnesses, asking for a continuance, vigorously cross-examining witnesses, questioning motives, highlighting testimonial inconsistencies, advising defendant on possible plea deals, pointing out flaws in the State's case to the jury, making a vigorous closing statement, and asking the judge for a directed verdict); Gochicoa v. Johnson, 238 F.3d 278, 285 (5th Cir. 2000) (rejecting district court's conclusion that counsel totally "abdicated his role in the adversarial process" and was "inert" and finding that because counsel "presented some meaningful assistance to [defendant]," *Strickland* rather than *Cronic* applied); Jones v. Jones, 163 F.3d 285, 300 (5th Cir. 1998) (counsel did not entirely fail to subject the State's case to meaningful adversarial testing and *Cronic* does not control where, among other things, counsel attempted to suppress evidence, objected at trial to the admission of evidence, and cross-examined the State's witnesses); Cooks v. Ward, 165 F.3d 1283, 1296 (10th Cir. 1998) (agreeing that counsel was ineffective during sentencing but finding his failures did not trigger a presumption of prejudice where counsel was present in the courtroom, conducted limited cross-examination, made evidentiary objections, and gave a closing argument).

162. 122 S. Ct. 1843 (2002).

163. *Id.* at 1851.

The Court went on to conclude that the conduct challenged in the case before it—failure to present mitigating evidence and waiver of closing argument—was similar to the other attorney errors to which *Strickland*, not *Cronic*, applies.[164]

[ii]   Prosecutor's Aide Cases

In *Cronic* the Court stated that "the adversarial process protected by the Sixth Amendment requires that the accused have 'counsel acting in the role of an advocate.'"[165] Consistent with this statement, some federal circuit courts have found Sixth Amendment violations in prosecutor's aide cases—cases in which counsel acts, but acts in a manner that aids the prosecutor rather than advocating for the defense. *United States v. Swanson*[166] is an example. In *Swanson*, defense counsel conceded, during closing argument, that no reasonable doubt existed regarding the only factual issues in dispute. The United States Court of Appeals for the Ninth Circuit held that counsel's concession constituted a constructive denial of counsel within the meaning of *Cronic*. The court reasoned that "[i]nstead of serving as his client's advocate during closing argument, [counsel] abandoned his client at a critical stage of the proceedings and affirmatively aided the prosecutor in her efforts to persuade the jury that there was no reasonable doubt."[167] The court found that counsel's concession caused a breakdown in the adversarial system and constituted an "utter[] fail[ure]" to subject the prosecution's case to meaningful adversarial testing.[168] The federal circuit courts, however, do not consistently treat admissions of guilt as constructive denials of counsel.[169] Of course, in North Carolina, a concession of guilt without the defendant's consent is per se ineffectiveness under *State v. Harbison*.[170]

[iii]   Combination Cases

Finally, some cases are best characterized as combination cases, where counsel failed to act on the defendant's behalf, and when counsel did act, he or she served as the prosecution's helper.[171]

---

164. *See id.* at 1851–52 (citing Darden v. Wainwright, 477 U.S. 168, 184 (1986) (evaluating claim that counsel was ineffective by failing to present mitigating evidence at capital sentencing under *Strickland*); Burger v. Kemp, 483 U.S. 776, 788 (1987) (same)).

165. *Cronic*, 466 U.S. at 656 (quoting Anders v. California, 386 U.S. 738, 743 (1967)).

166. 943 F.2d 1070 (9th Cir. 1991).

167. *Id.* at 1075.

168. *Id.* at 1074.

169. *See* Haynes v. Cain, 298 F.3d 375 (5th Cir. 2002) (holding that although counsel made an admission of guilt, counsel did not entirely fail to subject the State's case to meaningful adversarial testing and therefore *Strickland*, not *Cronic*, applied), *cert. denied*, 123 S. Ct. 676 (2002).

170. *See infra* pp. 48–49 (discussing *Harbison* claims in detail).

171. *See* Rickman v. Bell, 131 F.3d 1150, 1157 (6th Cir. 1997) ("[Counsel] combined a total failure to actively advocate his client's cause with repeated expressions of contempt for his client for his alleged actions. The effect of all this was to provide [the defendant] not with a defense counsel, but with a second prosecutor.").

Depending on the facts, another way of framing a claim alleging that counsel failed to subject the State's case to meaningful adversarial testing and acted instead as the prosecution's helper

[b]   Where No Lawyer Could Provide Effective Assistance

The *Cronic* Court identified circumstances where "the likelihood that any lawyer, even a fully competent one, could provide effective assistance is . . . small"[172] as falling within the scope of its rule and requiring a presumption of prejudice. The Court cited *Powell v. Alabama*[173] as a case falling in this category. In *Powell*, counsel, who had no time to prepare the defendant's capital case or familiarize himself with local procedure, was appointed on the day of trial. Although the Court has recognized that late appointment of counsel does not automatically require an application of the per se prejudice rule,[174] it held in *Powell* that counsel's appointment was "so close upon the trial as to amount to a denial of effective and substantial aid"[175] and required a presumption of prejudice.[176] Similar North Carolina cases can be found.[177]

Cronic itself contrasts with *Powell*, offering an example of a case where the surrounding circumstances were insufficient to warrant a presumption of prejudice. In *Cronic*, the defendant was indicted for mail fraud. Shortly before trial, retained counsel withdrew. The court appointed a young lawyer with a real estate practice to represent the defendant and allowed counsel twenty-five days to prepare for trial, notwithstanding the fact that the government had taken over four and a half years to investigate the case and had reviewed thousands of documents during its investigation. After being convicted, defendant appealed. The Sixth Circuit reversed, concluding that the circumstances

---

may be as a conflict of interest claim. *See infra* pp. 34–48 (discussing conflict of interest claims, including those where an attorney is burdened by a conflict between his client's interests and his own sympathies).

172. United States v. Cronic, 466 U.S. 648, 659–60 (1984).

173. 287 U.S. 45 (1932).

174. *See Cronic*, 466 U.S. at 661 ("But every refusal to postpone a criminal trial will not give rise to . . . a presumption [of prejudice]."); Chambers v. Maroney, 399 U.S. 42, 54 (1970) (Court was "not disposed to fashion a per se rule requiring reversal of every conviction following tardy appointment of counsel").

175. *Powell*, 287 U.S. at 53.

176. *See Cronic*, 466 U.S. at 660–61 (so characterizing *Powell*).

177. *See* State v. Pait, 81 N.C. App. 286, 290, 343 S.E.2d 573, 576 (1986) ("because of the unusual celerity with which the State and court moved defendant's counsel was not, and could not have possibly been, prepared to effectively advise and assist his client"); State v. Maher, 305 N.C. 544, 549, 290 S.E.2d 694, 697 (1982) ("where counsel is retained only four days prior to trial through no fault of defendant's, is concurrently involved in another trial, and is allowed only a few minutes to confer with his client prior to trial, failure of the trial court to grant a continuance denied defendant effective assistance of counsel"); State v. McFadden, 292 N.C. 609, 616, 234 S.E.2d 742, 747 (1977) (holding that denial of a motion to continue deprived defendant of his right to effective assistance because defendant and counsel had inadequate time to prepare for trial; defendant, who was charged with a felony, met and talked with counsel for the first time about ninety minutes before the case was called for trial, counsel had practiced law for only eighteen months and had tried only one jury case, and counsel knew nothing about the case until he arrived in court).

warranted an inference that counsel was unable to discharge his duties and thus the defendant was denied effective assistance. The Sixth Circuit found that this inference was warranted based on its use of five criteria: (1) the time afforded for investigation and preparation, (2) counsel's experience, (3) the gravity of the charge, (4) the complexity of the possible defenses, and (5) the accessibility of the witnesses. The Supreme Court reversed, finding that although these five factors are relevant to an evaluation of effectiveness, they "neither separately nor in combination . . . provide a basis for concluding that competent counsel was not able to provide this respondent with the guiding hand that the Constitution guarantees."[178]

The *Cronic* Court noted that although the trial court gave counsel only twenty-five days to prepare, counsel requested only thirty days to prepare. Also, the Court rejected the notion that either the disparity between the length of the government's investigation and the time afforded to counsel to prepare or the number of documents reviewed by the government deserved special weight. It held that neither of these facts was "necessarily relevant" to whether a competent lawyer could prepare the case in twenty-five days, because the government's task of proving that a defendant is guilty is "entirely different" from the defense's task in preparing to rebut the charge. The Court also found that the significance of counsel's preparation time was further reduced by the straightforward nature of the charges and the fact that the only bona fide issue in the case was whether respondent acted with intent to defraud. The Court went on state that its conclusion was not undermined by the counsel's youth or by the fact that his principal practice was real estate, noting that every experienced criminal lawyer once tried his or her first case. Finally, the Court rejected the other factors—gravity of the charge, complexity of the case, and accessibility of witnesses—finding that "none identifies circumstances that in themselves make it unlikely that respondent received the effective assistance of counsel."[179] It concluded that the surrounding circumstances did not warrant a presumption of prejudice and that, therefore, the defendant could make out a claim of ineffective assistance only by pointing to specific errors made by trial counsel.[180]

---

178. *Cronic*, 466 U.S. at 663.

179. *Id.* at 666.

180. *See id.*
The Fourth Circuit has noted that since 1984, when the United States Supreme Court articulated the tests for actual and per se prejudice in *Strickland* and *Cronic*, it has never once found per se prejudice under the "likelihood that any lawyer, even a fully competent one, could provide effective assistance" prong. *See* Glover v. Miro, 262 F.3d 268, 277 (4th Cir. 2001), *cert. denied*, 122 S. Ct. 1966 (2002). The Fourth Circuit itself repeatedly has rejected contentions that a presumption of prejudice applies under the "circumstances such that no lawyer could render effective assistance" test. *See id.* at 278–79 (rejecting claim where defendant met only briefly with original public defender assigned to his case, where new counsel did not receive the case file until the day the term of court for which defendant's case was scheduled began, new counsel was responsible for fifty or sixty other criminal cases at the time, and defendant was charged with serious crimes for which he claimed to have alibi witnesses); Griffin v. Aiken, 775 F.2d 1226, 1229–30 (4th Cir. 1985) (distinguishing *Powell* and finding no per se prejudice

The North Carolina Supreme Court has addressed a Sixth Amendment claim on analogous facts. In *State v. Tunstall*,[181] the defendant argued that the trial court's denial of his motion to continue deprived him of his right to effective assistance of counsel. Specifically, the defendant contended that a continuance was warranted based on his unavailability to counsel until the day before trial and the lateness of discovery provided by the State. The court rejected the defendant's argument, finding the facts did not support the defendant's claim that he was inaccessible to counsel. Acknowledging that the State provided tardy notice of certain oral statements made by the defendant, the court noted that counsel had three days between receiving notice and jury selection.

Tunstall noted two prior decisions holding that denials of motions to continue violated the defendants' Sixth Amendment rights. In one, *State v. McFadden*,[182] the felony defendant's retained counsel was not present when the case was called for trial. Counsel's junior associate appeared in court and requested a continuance on the basis that retained counsel was trying a case in federal court and was the only person prepared to try the defendant's case. The trial court denied the motion and ordered the junior associate to try the case. The junior associate had practiced law for only eighteen months, had tried only one jury case, knew nothing about the case before the day of trial, and had discussed the case with the defendant for only ninety minutes. On these facts, the North Carolina Supreme Court held that the defendant's Sixth Amendment right to counsel was violated because he and his counsel did not have a reasonable time in which to prepare and present a defense.

The second case noted by *Tunstall* was *State v. Maher*.[183] In *Maher*, the defendant's retained counsel prepared the case for trial but withdrew on November 19, at which time the defendant retained new counsel. After being informed the next day by the prosecutor that the case was scheduled for trial on November 24, an associate of the defendant's new counsel advised the court that new counsel was trying a case that was expected to last into the next week. The associate also moved for a continuance. The trial court denied the motion. When the case was called for trial on November 24, new counsel moved for a continuance on grounds of inadequate trial preparation, indicating that he had not yet talked to the defendant. The trial court denied the motion and gave counsel fifteen minutes to consult with the defendant. On these facts, the

---

where defendant alleged minimal pre-indictment investigation by counsel, continuous presence of counsel in court on other matters in the three-day period between indictment and trial, counsel's failure to obtain a transcript of the hearing, limited time to speak with counsel in the period between the preliminary hearing and the morning of trial, the inability of counsel appointed on the day before trial to present constitutional grounds for the suppression of evidence since counsel had no knowledge of the facts, and the fact that defendant's public defender had between 100 and 140 other pending cases at the time); Praylow v. Martin, 761 F.2d 179, 181–83 (4th Cir. 1985) (no per se prejudice where counsel was appointed one day after indictment and on the day of trial).

181. 334 N.C. 320, 432 S.E.2d 331 (1993).

182. 292 N.C. 609, 234 S.E.2d 742 (1977).

183. 305 N.C. 544, 290 S.E.2d 694 (1982).

North Carolina Supreme Court held that the trial court's denial of the motion to continue violated the defendant's Sixth Amendment right to counsel.

After *Tunsall*, the North Carolina Supreme Court decided *State v. Rogers*.[184] In that case, the trial court granted the capital defendant's pretrial motion to dismiss his retained counsel. After the defendant was unable to retain new counsel, the trial court appointed new lead counsel and, one day later, appointed co-counsel. The defendant's trial was scheduled to begin in thirty-four days. Twenty-three days after being appointed, new counsel moved for a continuance and to withdraw on grounds that there was no possibility that they could be fully prepared for trial. Both motions were denied. A week later, new counsel again unsuccessfully moved for a continuance. The defendant was convicted and sentenced to death. The defendant appealed, arguing that the trial court's denials of his requests for continuances resulted in a violation of his constitutional right to effective assistance of counsel. The North Carolina Supreme Court agreed.

On the issue of whether a violation of the defendant's Sixth Amendment right to counsel had occurred, the court noted that to prevail, the defendant must show that he did not have ample time to confer with counsel and to investigate, prepare, and present his defense. The court found this standard satisfied, stating:

> After a thorough review of the record, we are convinced that defendant's counsel
> had insufficient time to prepare for the defense of this case. While it is clear that
> defendant's prior counsel . . . filed most of the usual pretrial motions, it is equally
> clear that there was little or no trial preparation conducted before [he] was dis-
> missed. There was no evidence that any witness interviews had been performed.
> The orders based on the trial court's rulings on pretrial motions had not been pre-
> pared. A jury questionnaire was not submitted for distribution to prospective
> jurors even though requested by defendant's prior counsel and allowed by the trial
> court. [New counsel] were appointed to a case involving multiple incidents in
> multiple locations over a two-day period for which they had only thirty-four days
> to prepare. It is unreasonable to expect that any attorney, no matter his or her
> level of experience, could be adequately prepared to conduct a bifurcated capital
> trial for a case as complex and involving as many witnesses as the instant case.[185]

Citing *Tunstall*, *Maher*, and *Cronic*, the court held that where, as in the case before it, the likelihood that any lawyer could provide assistance is remote, prejudice must be presumed.[186]

---

184. 352 N.C. 119, 529 S.E.2d 671 (2000).

185. 352 N.C. at 125, 529 S.E.2d at 675–76.

186. The *Rogers* court was careful to note that the courts do not deny constitutional rights "just because they act expeditiously," 352 N.C. at 126, 529 S.E.2d at 676 (quotation omitted), and that it would "vigilantly resist any manipulation by parties or their counsel . . . to disrupt or obstruct the orderly process of the court." *Id.* (quotation omitted).

§ 1.05 Conflict of Interest Claims

The constitutional right to effective assistance of counsel includes the right to counsel unimpaired by competing loyalties.[187] This principle gives rise to what this book refers to as conflict of interest claims. Conflict of interest claims are a special category of IAC claims that are not governed by the *Strickland* analysis.

The potential for competing loyalties, and thus a conflict of interest, can arise in a number of situations. Many allegations of conflict of interest arise in multiple representation situations, where one counsel represents two or more codefendants.[188] Other situations that can lead to a conflict of interest include, for example, those where counsel represents the defendant and a prosecution witness,[189] where counsel represents the defendant and the prosecutor or the victim,[190] where counsel is implicated in the criminal activity that resulted in the charges against the defendant,[191] or where counsel's fee is paid by a third party.[192]

---

187. *See* Wood v. Georgia, 450 U.S. 261, 271 (1981) ("Where a constitutional right to counsel exists, our Sixth Amendment cases hold that there is a correlative right to representation that is free from conflicts of interest."); Cuyler v. Sullivan, 446 U.S. 335 (1980); Holloway v. Arkansas, 435 U.S. 475 (1978); State v. Bruton, 344 N.C. 381, 391, 474 S.E.2d 336, 343 (1996) (the right to effective assistance of counsel includes the "'right to representation that is free from conflicts of interest'") (quoting *Wood*, 450 U.S. at 271); State v. Hardison, 143 N.C. App. 114, 120, 545 S.E.2d 233, 237 (2001) ("A criminal defendant has a constitutional right to effective assistance of counsel, which includes the right to representation that is free from conflicts of interest.") (quotations omitted); State v. Asenault, 46 N.C. App. 7, 13, 264 S.E.2d 592, 596 (1980) ("a defendant has a constitutional right to the undivided loyalty of his counsel").

188. *See Holloway*, 435 U.S. 475 (impermissible conflict due to multiple representation); *Cuyler*, 466 U.S. 335 (allegation of conflict due to multiple representation); *Bruton*, 344 N.C. at 390–92, 474 S.E.2d at 343–44 (same); State v. Winslow, 97 N.C. App. 551, 556, 389 S.E.2d 436, 439–40 (1990) (same); State v. Yelton, 87 N.C. App. 554, 361 S.E.2d 753 (1987) (same).
A division of loyalties also can occur when two lawyers at the same law firm represent two or more codefendants. *See Arsenault*, 46 N.C. App. at 13–14, 264 S.E.2d at 596 ("Where two members of the same law firm serve as counsel for codefendants with conflicting interests, a division of loyalties occurs. For constitutional purposes, it is as though only one counsel was involved.") (citations omitted).

189. *See* State v. James, 111 N.C. App. 785, 433 S.E.2d 755 (1993), *aff'd*, 122 S. Ct. 1237 (2002).

190. *See, e.g.*, Mickens v. Taylor, 240 F.3d 348 (4th Cir. 2001), *aff'd*, 122 S. Ct. 1237 (2002).

191. *See, e.g.*, State v. Loye, 56 N.C. App. 501, 289 S.E.2d 860 (1982) (conflict of interest existed where counsel was indicted for crime involving the defendant).

192. *See, e.g.*, Wood v. Georgia, 450 U.S. 261, 267–70 (1981) (recognizing risk of conflict of interest where defendants were represented by attorney paid for by their employer). *See generally* LaFave, *supra* note 2, § 11.9(a) (discussing the range of possible conflicts of interest that may develop).

The mere potential for a conflict of interest does not by itself rise to the level of a Sixth Amendment violation. Were that so, the common practice of joint representation of codefendants would per se violate the constitution. The United States Supreme Court has rejected that approach, requiring in all cases that more be shown than the mere potential for conflict of interest.[193]

As illustrated by Table 5, the standard that applies to a Sixth Amendment conflict of interest claim depends on the procedural context in which the claim arises. The sections that follow discuss the different procedural contexts in which conflict of interest claims arise and the standards that apply to each.

Table 5: Conflict of Interest Claims

Procedural Context	Applicable Standard
Conflict is raised before or during trial	*Holloway*
All other cases	*Cuyler*

---

[1]   Where the Defendant Raises the Conflict before or during Trial

One procedural context in which conflict of interest claims arise is when defense counsel timely raises a conflict of interest with the trial court. Claims arising in this procedural context are governed by the United States Supreme Court's decision in *Holloway v. Arkansas*.[194]

[a]   The *Holloway* Rule

In *Holloway*, a single public defender represented three codefendants in a joint trial. Notwithstanding the public defender's repeated objections that the joint representation created a conflict of interest, the trial court declined to inquire about the conflict. After being convicted, the defendant appealed. The United States Supreme Court reversed, holding that a defendant's right to effective assistance of counsel is violated when in the face of a timely defense objection on grounds of conflict, the trial court fails "either to appoint separate counsel or to take adequate steps to ascertain whether the risk was too remote to warrant separate counsel."[195] The Court further held that when such a failure occurs, reversal is automatic; no showing of prejudice is required.[196] Finally, the

---

193. *See Holloway*, 435 U.S. at 482 ("Requiring or permitting a single attorney to represent codefendants . . . is not *per se* violative of constitutional guarantees of effective assistance of counsel."); *see also Bruton*, 344 N.C. at 391, 474 S.E.2d at 343 ("Permitting a single attorney to represent two or more codefendants in the same trial is not a *per se* violation of the right to effective assistance of counsel."). The United States Supreme Court has recognized that in some cases, codefendants benefit from joint representation: "Joint representation is a means of insuring against reciprocal recrimination. A common defense often gives strength against a common attack." *Holloway*, 435 U.S. at 482–83 (quotation omitted).

194. 435 U.S. 475 (1978).

195. *Id*. at 484.

196. *See id*. at 488 ("whenever a trial court improperly requires joint representation over timely objection reversal is automatic"); *see also* Mickens v. Taylor, 122 S. Ct. 1237, 1238 (2002) ("*Holloway* . . . creates an automatic reversal rule only where defense counsel is forced

Holloway Court confirmed that where inquiry is made and a conflict is found, a defendant may waive the right to counsel unimpeded by a conflict of interest.[197]

[b] The *Holloway* Inquiry and the Required Response

Holloway imposes an obligation on the trial court to inquire when a conflict of interest is timely raised by defense counsel. The trial court's inquiry must be "full and searching" and may include *in camera* proceedings or discussions between the trial judge and the defendant or defendants.[198] But what is the court looking for? In *Holloway*, the Supreme Court reversed on the ground that the trial court failed to ascertain whether the risk associated with the conflict of interest was "too remote to warrant separate counsel."[199] The Court noted that the lower courts had split on how strong a showing of conflict must be made.[200] The Court found it unnecessary to resolve this conflict, because it was clear in the case before it that the trial court failed to afford defense counsel an opportunity to do anything other than make conclusory representations about the conflict.[201] *Holloway* thus left the lower courts with only a vague admonition that they must ascertain whether the risk is "too remote to warrant separate counsel." Later decisions have not clarified this standard.[202]

It is clear, however, that a timely objection on grounds of conflict triggers the duty to inquire. The inquiry may reveal a potential or actual conflict. An actual conflict would exist, for example, when counsel represents codefendants and each intends to assert defenses exculpating himself or herself and inculpating the other. More common than actual conflicts are potential conflicts. Conflicts present more commonly as potential rather than actual for two reasons. First, attorney–client privilege or ethical rules may prevent defense counsel from revealing the details necessary to substantiate a finding of an actual conflict.[203] Second, when the objection is raised before trial, the court must rule on the issue "not with the wisdom of hindsight" after a trial "but in the murkier pre-trial context when relationships between parties are seen through a glass, darkly."[204] The United States Supreme Court has noted:

---

to represent codefendants over his timely objection, unless the trial court has determined that there is no conflict.").

197. *See Holloway*, 435 U.S. at 483 n.5.

198. State v. Yelton, 87 N.C. App. 554, 557, 361 S.E.2d 753, 756 (1987).

199. *Holloway*, 435 U.S. at 484.

200. *See id.* at 483.

201. *See id.* at 484 & n.7.

202. *See* Wheat v. United States, 486 U.S. 153, 160 (1988) (noting that *Holloway* held that "a court confronted with and alerted to possible conflicts of interest must take adequate steps to ascertain whether the conflicts warrant separate counsel"). *But see* Mickens v. Taylor, 122 S. Ct. 1237 (2002) (a case that could be read as indicating that if an inquiry is held and only a potential conflict is found, the automatic reversal rule will not apply even if the trial court neither appoints new counsel nor obtains a waiver).

203. *See Holloway*, 435 U.S. at 487 (recognizing that confidential communications may inhibit disclosure).

204. *Wheat*, 486 U.S. at 162.

The likelihood and dimensions of nascent conflicts of interest are notoriously hard to predict, even for those thoroughly familiar with criminal trials. It is a rare attorney who will be fortunate enough to learn the entire truth from his own client, much less be fully apprised before trial of what each of the Government's witnesses will say on the stand. A few bits of unforeseen testimony or a single previously unknown or unnoticed document may significantly shift the relationship between multiple defendants.[205]

Another point that is clear is that once the requisite quantum of conflict is found, the trial court must either disqualify counsel or obtain a waiver from the defendant. To be valid, a waiver must be made knowingly and voluntarily.[206] In *Wheat v. United*

---

205. *Id.* at 162–63.

206. *See* State v. James, 111 N.C. App. 785, 791–92, 433 S.E.2d 755, 759 (1993) ("the Sixth Amendment right to conflict-free representation can be waived by a defendant, if done knowingly, intelligently and voluntarily"); State v. Yelton, 87 N.C. App. 554, 557, 361 S.E.2d 753, 756 (1987) (defendants made knowing, intelligent, and voluntary waivers).

In *Yelton*, 87 N.C. App. 554, 361 S.E.2d 753, a case involving multiple representation, the court set out the requisite inquiry for determining whether a waiver is knowing, intelligent, and voluntary. First, the court held, there must be evidence on the issue of the defendants' consent to joint representation and the defendants' consent must have been based upon a full disclosure of the advantages and disadvantages of such representation. 87 N.C. App. at 557, 361 S.E.2d at 756. Further, the court held, the defendants must be aware that their insistence upon joint representation may constitute a waiver of their right to later argue that they were denied effective assistance of counsel because of conflict of interest. *See id.* The court went on to find instructive an inquiry adopted by the United States Court of Appeals for the Fifth Circuit. Under that procedure the court

> should address each defendant personally and forthrightly advise him of the potential dangers of representation by counsel with a conflict of interest. The defendant must be at liberty to question the . . . court as to the nature and consequences of his legal representation. Most significantly, the court should seek to elicit a narrative response from each defendant that he has been advised of his right to effective representation, that he understands the details of his attorney's possible conflict of interest and the potential perils of such a conflict, that he has discussed the matter with his attorney or if he wishes with outside counsel, and that he voluntarily waives his Sixth Amendment protections.

87 N.C. App. at 558, 361 S.E.2d at 756–57 (quoting United States v. Garcia, 517 F.2d 272, 278 (5th Cir. 1975), *abrogated on other grounds*, Flanagan v. United States, 465 U.S. 259 (1984). The *Yelton* court went on to hold that in the case before it, there was "substantial compliance" with this inquiry and that the defendants voluntarily, knowingly, and intelligently waived the right to appeal on grounds of IAC based on their lawyer's potential conflict of interest. 87 N.C. App. at 559, 361 S.E.2d at 757; *see also* State v. Bruton, 344 N.C. 381, 390–91, 474 S.E.2d 336, 343 (1996) (noting that at pretrial hearing on conflict of interest, (1) the trial court informed both defendants that a conflict could possibly arise, that each had a right to his own lawyer, and that a future course of action might advantage one defendant and disadvantage another, (2) both defendants assented to the joint representation, and (3) the trial court found no actual conflict and both defendants waived their right to separate counsel). For another North Carolina decision on waiver of counsel,

States,[207] the United States Supreme Court held that in both the "rare case" where an actual conflict is discerned and in the more common instance where only a potential conflict appears, the trial court has "substantial latitude" to refuse to accept a waiver and insist that the defendant obtain or be appointed new counsel.[208] This holding gives the trial court broad discretion to disqualify counsel instead of accepting a waiver where an actual or potential conflict is found.

Although not required, it may be prudent in all cases for the trial court to inquire before trial about any possible conflicts of interest.[209] And, under *Holloway*, the trial court should make inquiry and obtain a waiver or require new counsel whenever a timely objection is made and conflict in fact appears.

[c]   Scope of the *Holloway* Rule

Holloway involved a conflict of interest stemming from multiple representation. Since *Holloway*, lower courts have routinely applied its automatic reversal rule to conflicts of interests other than those stemming from multiple representation.[210] Although

---

see State v. Fulp, 355 N.C. 171, 558 S.E.2d 156 (2002) (trial court's findings show that defendant was aware of his right to counsel, understood and appreciated the consequences of his decision, and knowingly, intelligently, and voluntarily waived his right to counsel).

207. 486 U.S. 153, 162–64 (1988).

208. *Id.* at 163.

209. *See* Mickens v. Taylor, 122 S. Ct. 1237, 1244 (2002) (conflict law "which requires proof of effect upon representation but (once such effect is shown) presumes prejudice . . . creates an 'incentive' to inquire into a potential conflict"); *see also* State v. Arsenault, 46 N.C. App. 7, 14, 264 S.E.2d 592, 596 (1980) ("[T]he instant case points out the need for the trial judge to inquire prior to trial about possible conflicts of interest arising from joint representation of codefendants by members of the same law firm or by single joint counsel."); Burger v. Kemp, 483 U.S. 776, 800 (1987) (Blackmun, J., dissenting) ("A judge can avoid the problem by questioning the defendant, at an early stage in the criminal process, in any case presenting a situation that may give rise to conflict, in order to determine whether the defendant is aware of the possible conflict and whether he has waived his right to conflict-free representation."). This is in fact the practice in federal court. *See* FED. R. CRIM. P. 44(c). Federal Rule of Criminal Procedure 44(c) now provides that whenever two or more defendants have been jointly charged or joined for trial and are represented by the same counsel or counsel who are associated in the practice of law,

> the court shall promptly inquire with respect to such joint representation and shall personally advise each defendant of the right to the effective assistance of counsel, including separate representation. Unless it appears that there is good cause to believe no conflict of interest is likely to arise, the court shall take such measures as may be appropriate to protect each defendant's right to counsel.

210. *See, e.g.*, Spreitzer v. Peters, 114 F.3d 1435, 1451 n.7 (7th Cir. 1997) ("we have routinely applied . . . *Holloway* . . . to conflict of interest cases which are not multiple representation cases, and we do so here"); United States v. Cook, 45 F.3d 388, 393 (10th Cir. 1995) ("Although *Holloway* was a multiple representation case, the district court's duty of inquiry 'arise[s] whenever there is the possibility that a criminal defendant's attorney suffers from any sort of conflict of interest.'") (quoting United States v. Levy, 25 F.3d 146, 153 (2d Cir. 1994)).

the North Carolina appellate courts have not decided whether *Holloway* extends beyond multiple representation situations, the court of appeals has extended the closely related *Cuyler* rule beyond those situations. While such decisions might be read as suggesting that the court would extend *Holloway*[211] in a similar fashion, that view may be tempered by recent dictum from the United States Supreme Court indicating that application of the related *Cuyler* rule[212] beyond the multiple representation context may have been unwarranted.[213]

[d]   Timing of the *Holloway* Objection

Although the United States Supreme Court indicated that a *Holloway* objection must be "timely,"[214] it did not define that term.[215] It did, however, indicate that courts should not allow defense counsel to interpose an untimely conflict of interest objection for "dilatory purposes."[216] The North Carolina appellate courts have not had occasion to rule on the meaning of the term "timely" or on the standard for determining whether an objection was made for dilatory purposes.

[e]   North Carolina Cases Applying *Holloway*

There are no North Carolina cases applying the *Holloway* rule to require reversal where the defendant made an objection and the trial court failed to conduct the requisite inquiry.[217]

[2]   Where the Conflict Is Not Raised until after Conviction

Another procedural context in which conflict of interest claims arise is where defense counsel makes no objection before or during trial regarding a conflict, where the trial court has no reason to believe that a conflict exists, and where the defendant later challenges his or her conviction on grounds of conflict of interest. This category of cases is governed by the United States Supreme Court's decision in *Cuyler v. Sullivan*.[218]

But see Beets v. Scott, 65 F.3d 1258, 1265 (5th Cir. 1995) (declining to extend United States Supreme Court conflict of interest cases beyond the context of multiple or serial representation).

211. *See infra* pp. 44–46 (discussing and citing North Carolina cases that extended the *Cuyler* rule beyond multiple representation conflicts of interest).

212. *See infra* pp. 40–48 (discussing the *Cuyler* rule).

213. *See infra* p. 44 (discussing dictum in *Mickens v. Taylor*, 122 S. Ct. 1237 (2002)).

214. *See Holloway*, 435 U.S. at 488 ("whenever a trial court improperly requires joint representation over timely objection reversal is automatic").

215. In fact, in *Holloway*, the Court expressly reserved the issue of the constitutional significance of an objection not raised until midtrial. *See id.* at 484 n.7 (noting that the Court had "no occasion in this case to determine the constitutional significance, if any, of the trial court's response to petitioners' midtrial objections").

216. *Id.* at 486–87 ("When an untimely motion for separate counsel is made for dilatory purposes, our holding does not impair the trial court's ability to deal with counsel who resort to such tactics.").

217. However, the North Carolina courts have applied the rule in other contexts. *See, e.g.*, State v. Walls, 342 N.C. 1, 39–40, 463 S.E.2d 738, 757–58 (1995) (prosecutor raised conflict issue; adequate inquiry made).

218. 446 U.S. 335 (1980).

[a] The *Cuyler* Rule

In *Cuyler*, the defendant could not afford to pay for his own lawyer and accepted representation by attorneys who were representing his codefendants. At no time did the defendant or his lawyers object to the multiple representation. The defendant and his codefendants were tried separately; only the defendant was convicted. The defendant then challenged his conviction, asserting that he was denied effective assistance of counsel because of attorney conflict of interest stemming from the multiple representation.

The *Cuyler* Court noted that the defendant's claim raised two issues expressly reserved in *Holloway*: (1) whether a state trial judge must inquire into the propriety of multiple representation even though no party makes any objections; and (2) whether the mere possibility of a conflict of interest warrants the conclusion that the defendant was deprived of his right to counsel.[219] Turning to the first issue, the Court held that "[a]bsent special circumstances, . . . trial courts may assume either that multiple representation entails no conflict or that the lawyer and his clients knowingly accept such risk of conflict as may exist."[220] The Court continued, holding that "[u]nless the trial court knows or reasonably should know that a particular conflict exists, the court need not initiate an inquiry."[221] Applying that holding, the Court found that nothing in the case before it indicated that the trial court had a duty to inquire about a conflict of interest.[222]

Regarding the second issue—whether the mere possibility of a conflict of interest warrants the conclusion that the defendant was deprived of his right to counsel—the Court held that in order to establish a Sixth Amendment violation, a defendant who failed to object at trial must show that "an actual conflict of interest adversely affected his lawyer's performance."[223] Once this showing is made, a defendant need not demonstrate prejudice.[224]

---

219. *See* 446 U.S. at 345.

220. *Id.* at 346–47.

221. *Id.* at 347. The Court later expressly distinguished a situation when "the trial court knows or reasonably should know that a particular conflict exists" from one "when the trial court is aware of a vague, unspecified possibility of conflict, such as that which inheres in almost every instance of multiple representation." Mickens v. Taylor, 122 S. Ct. 1237, 1242 (2002).

222. *See Cuyler*, 466 U.S. at 347. Specifically, the Court noted that the fact that separate trials were held "significantly reduced the potential for a divergence in their interests." *Id.* Additionally, it noted that (1) no participant in the defendant's trial ever objected on grounds of conflict; (2) counsel's opening argument described a defense consistent with the view that none of the defendants was involved with the crimes and suggested counsel was not hesitant to call witnesses who might be needed at the codefendants' trials; and (3) counsel's decision to rest defendant's defense was a reasonable tactical response to a weak prosecution case. *See id.*

223. *Id.* at 348; *see* State v. Bruton, 344 N.C. 381, 391, 474 S.E.2d 336, 343 (1996) (same); State v. Hardison, 143 N.C. App. 114, 120, 545 S.E.2d 233, 237 (2001) (same); State v. Winslow, 97 N.C. App. 551, 556, 389 S.E.2d 436, 439 (1990) (same).

224. *Cuyler*, 466 U.S. at 349–50.

The *Cuyler* Court went on to discuss *Glasser v. United States*,[225] a case it characterized as satisfying the Court's test of actual conflict of interest adversely affecting performance. In *Glasser*, defense counsel represented codefendants at a joint trial. Counsel failed to cross-examine a prosecution witness whose testimony linked the defendant with the crime and failed to object to the presentation of arguably inadmissible evidence. Both omissions resulted from counsel's desire to diminish the jury's perception of a codefendant's guilt. Because the actual conflict of interest impaired the defendant's defense, the Court reversed his conviction.

The *Cuyler* Court then offered *Dukes v. Warden*[226] as a "contrasting situation," where the actual conflict of interest adversely affecting performance test was not satisfied. In *Dukes*, the defendant pleaded guilty on the recommendation of two lawyers, one of whom also represented the defendant's codefendants on an unrelated charge. The defendant then learned that this lawyer had sought leniency for the codefendants, arguing that their cooperation with the police induced the defendant to plead guilty. The *Cuyler* Court noted that in *Dukes*, nothing indicated that the alleged conflict of interest rendered the plea involuntary and unintelligent; since the defendant did not identify "an actual lapse in representation," the Court affirmed the denial of post-conviction relief.[227]

Turning to the case before it, the *Cuyler* Court noted that the lower court had granted the defendant relief because he had shown that the multiple representation involved a possible conflict of interest. The Court rejected this holding, stating that the possibility of conflict "is insufficient to impugn a criminal conviction" and reiterating that in this context, a defendant must show that an actual conflict of interest adversely affected counsel's performance.[228] The Court then remanded for a determination of whether that standard was met.

[b]   Applying the *Cuyler* Rule

Cuyler's actual conflict of interest adversely affecting performance test has not been easy to apply. The Supreme Court's decision in *Burger v. Kemp*,[229] handed down seven years after *Cuyler*, is illustrative. In *Burger*, the defendant was represented by attorney Leaphart, tried in state court, found guilty of murder, and sentenced to death. The defendant's accomplice, Stevens, was tried separately. The defendant challenged his conviction in federal court, asserting, in part, that he was denied his right to effective assistance of counsel because of attorney conflict of interest. Specifically, he argued that Leaphart's partner, Robert Smith, was appointed to represent Stevens in his separate trial for the same murder.

The Court held that the mere overlap of counsel did not by itself constitute an actual conflict of interest.[230] It went on to reject the defendant's argument that an actual

---

225. 315 U.S. 60 (1942).

226. 406 U.S. 250 (1972).

227. *Cuyler*, 446 U.S. at 349.

228. *Id.* at 350.

229. 483 U.S. 776 (1987).

230. *See id.* at 783–84.

conflict of interest was created when Leaphart prepared appellate briefs for both the defendant and Stevens and failed to argue lesser culpability on the defendant's behalf. The Court held that Leaphart's decision to forgo this argument had a sound strategic basis because the defendant had actually killed the victim and his actions had been found to be vile and inhuman.[231] The Court further held that "determining that there was an actual conflict of interest requires the attribution of Leaphart's motivation for not making the 'lesser culpability' argument to the fact that his partner was Stevens's lawyer, or to the further fact that he assisted his partner in that representation."[232] The Court adopted the lower court's finding that no such linkage was established.

The Court then went on to hold that even if an actual conflict had been established, it did not harm defense counsel's advocacy. Specifically, the Court rejected the defendant's argument that the joint representation caused Leaphart to fail to negotiate a plea and to take advantage of the defendant's lesser culpability, finding neither argument supported by the record.[233] On the plea agreement argument, the Court credited Leaphart's testimony that he tried to negotiate a plea but was rebuffed. Rejecting the lesser culpability argument, the Court noted that the argument might have been more persuasive if the defendants had been tried together. Because they were tried separately, the Court concluded that Leaphart "would have had no particular reason for concern about the possible impact of the tactics in [the defendant's] trial on the outcome of Stevens's trial."[234] Additionally, Leaphart testified that he did not try to protect Stevens, and the record indicated he tried to portray Stevens as more culpable than the defendant.

Justice Blackmun, joined by Justices Brennan and Marshall, dissented, finding "no doubt" that Leaphart "actively represented conflicting interests."[235] According to Justice Blackmun, the two lawyers assisted in the preparation of both cases; Smith sat with Leaphart at the defendant's trial and helped him; the prosecutor viewed them as joint counsel; and Smith was listed as the defendant's counsel on the trial transcript. Although Leaphart did not assist in Stevens's trial, he helped with pretrial research and strategy, conducted interviews of Stevens, and prepared the appellate briefs for both defendants. Justice Blackmun found that the codefendant's interests "were diametrically opposed" on the "crucial" issue of comparative culpability[236] and that this conflict caused Leaphart to abandon the lesser culpability argument in the defendant's appellate brief and fail to offer the defendant's testimony against Stevens during plea negotiations.[237] Specifically, he concluded that professional responsibility precluded Leaphart from pursuing lesser culpability in the defendant's appellate

---

231. *See id.* at 784.

232. *Id.* at 784–85.

233. *See id.* at 785.

234. *Burger*, 483 U.S. at 786.

235. *See id.* at 801 (Blackmum, J., dissenting).

236. *Id.* at 802.

237. *See id.* at 806–07.

brief.[238] This fact, he found, "compels" a conclusion that Leaphart's representation had an adverse effect on his performance.[239] He went on to conclude that the dual representation placed Leaphart in an "untenable" position during plea bargaining because he "was not in a position to negotiate . . . to the detriment of Stevens."[240]

Burger's majority and dissenting opinions illustrate the deceptive simplicity of the *Cuyler* test. After *Cuyler*, the lower courts struggled with its application, rightly noting that the elements of its test are "rather vague."[241] Some lower courts and commentators had interpreted *Cuyler* as setting forth a two-pronged test that required first, a showing of actual conflict and second, a showing of adverse affect.[242] They then struggled to define these terms. One difficulty in formulating the required definitions was delineating the difference between prejudice and adverse effect.[243] Because *Cuyler* held that prejudice is presumed once a defendant satisfies the *Cuyler* test, it was clear that adverse effect must differ from prejudice. *Cuyler* did not, however, clarify how the terms differ.

In fact, clarification did not come until 2002, more than twenty years later. In *Mickens v. Taylor*,[244] Justice Scalia, writing for the Court in a 5-4 decision, stated that the *Cuyler* test "is not properly read as requiring inquiry into actual conflict as something separate and apart from adverse effect."[245] He continued: "An 'actual conflict,' for Sixth Amendment purposes, is a conflict of interest that adversely affects counsel's performance."[246] This dictum indicates that the term "actual conflict" is synonymous with a conflict that adversely affects performance. While *Mickens* clarified that the *Cuyler* test has only one prong, not two, it complicated matters with regard to the meaning of the phrase "adversely affects counsel's performance." At one point in the opinion, the Court reformulates this phrase as "significantly affect[ing] counsel's performance—thereby rendering the verdict unreliable, even though *Strickland* prejudice cannot be shown."[247] Later, the Court seems to equate the meaning of the phrase with "defective performance."[248] Justice Kennedy's concurring opinion, which was

---

238. *See Burger*, 483 U.S. at 806 ("It would have been inconsistent with his duty of loyalty to Stevens to argue that the . . . [c]ourt should reduce [the defendant's] sentence . . . because Stevens was the more culpable defendant.").

239. *Id*. at 807.

240. *Id*.

241. Beets v. Scott, 65 F.3d 1258, 1265 (5th Cir. 1995).

242. *See* Note, *Conflicts of Interest in the Representation of Multiple Criminal Defendants: Clarifying* Cuyler v. Sullivan, 70 Geo. L. J. 1527, 1537–40 (1982).

243. *See id*. at 1539, 1541.

244. 122 S. Ct. 1237 (2002).

245. *Id*. at 1244 n.5.

246. *Id*.

247. *Id*. at 1244.

248. *Id*. at 1245.

joined by Justice O'Connor, describes the test as "whether trial counsel had a conflict of interest that hampered the representation."[249] Thus, even after *Mickens*, ambiguity remains.

[c] Scope of the *Cuyler* Rule

Another question that has arisen is whether *Cuyler* should apply only to multiple representation conflicts of interest or whether it should extend to other conflicts as well. At least one court has held that *Cuyler* is limited to multiple representation conflicts, with *Strickland* applying to all other conflicts.[250] However, the majority of courts—including those in North Carolina[251]—have applied *Cuyler* to other conflicts, without discussion.[252] In *Mickens v. Taylor*,[253] the United States Supreme Court expressly declined to rule on *Cuyler*'s applicability outside of the multiple representation context.[254] In his majority opinion, Justice Scalia noted, however, that the language of that case "does not clearly establish, or indeed even support"[255] application to other contexts, thus perhaps previewing how the Court might rule on the issue.

[d] North Carolina Cases Applying *Cuyler*

The North Carolina appellate courts have neither grappled with nor seemed to recognize the ambiguity inherent in the *Cuyler* test or the question of the proper scope of its application.[256] While a number of North Carolina decisions have rejected *Cuyler* claims,[257] at least two have found the claims to have merit. Both cases extend application of the *Cuyler* test beyond the multiple representation context.

---

249. *Mickens*, 122 S. Ct. at 1247 (Kennedy, J., concurring).

250. *See* Beets v. Scott, 65 F.3d 1258, 1265 (5th Cir. 1995).

251. *See, e.g.*, State v. James, 111 N.C. App. 785, 433 S.E.2d 755 (1993) (counsel represented the defendant and a prosecution witness); State v. Loye, 56 N.C. App. 501, 504, 289 S.E.2d 860, 862–63 (1982) (counsel was under investigation for his own participation in criminal conduct involving defendant).

252. *See Beets*, 65 F.3d at 1265–66 & n.10 (noting that lower courts have "unblinkingly" applied *Cuyler* beyond the multiple representation context and that "their decisions have not grappled with the difficulties inherent in that position").

253. 122 S. Ct. 1237 (2002).

254. *See id.* at 1246. ("In resolving this case on the grounds on which it was presented to us, we do not rule upon the need for the [*Cuyler* rule] . . . in cases of successive representation.")

255. *Id.* at 1245.

256. *See, e.g.*, State v. Hardison, 143 N.C. App. 114, 120, 545 S.E.2d 233, 237 (2001) (applying the *Cuyler* test and seeming to equate prejudice with adverse affect: "Defendant offered no evidence . . . to show that he was prejudiced or adversely affected in any manner by [the conflict]."); State v. Winslow, 97 N.C. App. 551, 556, 389 S.E.2d 436, 439–40 (1990) (without discussion, equating adverse impact with prejudice: "we are not persuaded by the argument that defendants were prejudiced by having one attorney who did not present these defenses"); State v. Willis, 61 N.C. App. 244, 249, 300 S.E.2d 829, 833 (1983) (same).

257. *See* State v. Bruton, 344 N.C. 381, 390–92, 474 S.E.2d 336, 343–44 (1996) (holding that the defendant failed to show that counsel's failure to challenge a codefendant's testimony "actually impaired [defendant's] defense"); State v. Walls, 342 N.C. 1, 40–41,

In *State v. James*,[258] the defendant, represented by attorney Hatfield, was convicted of second-degree murder. Before trial, Hatfield received a list of the State's witnesses. One of those witnesses was Haywood Parker, a client of Hatfield's in an unrelated matter. On appeal, the defendant argued that Hatfield's simultaneous representation of him and of the State's witness violated his right to effective assistance of counsel. The court agreed, finding the *Cuyler* test satisfied and ordering a new trial. It stated:

> We find the overlap of representation prior to and at the time of trial of both parties by attorney Hatfield resulted in an unavoidable conflict as to confidential communications, and affected counsel's ability to effectively impeach the credibility of witness Parker, thus compromising defendant's representation. A further example is that Parker's suggested plea bargain arrangement was never explored by defendant's counsel on cross-examination; this is in contrast to the suggested plea bargain arrangement of witness Timothy Cole which was vigorously attacked by counsel.[259]

In the second case, *State v. Loye*,[260] the defendant was indicted for armed robbery and pleaded not guilty. The defendant was represented at trial by attorneys Dailey and Vann. After trial began, the defendant followed his attorneys' advice and pleaded guilty. Shortly after the defendant was sentenced, Dailey was indicted for felonious receiving

---

463 S.E.2d 738, 758 (1995) (holding that even if defense counsel actively represented conflicting interests, defendant did not show that the dual representation actually affected the adequacy of his representation; conflict arose from fact that one of defendant's lawyers had represented a prosecution witness); *Hardison*, 143 N.C. App. at 120–21, 545 S.E.2d at 237 ("Defendant offered no evidence . . . to show that he was prejudiced or adversely affected in any manner by any friendship or acquaintanceship which [his counsel] may have had with [the victims]."); *Winslow*, 97 N.C. App. at 556, 389 S.E.2d at 439–40 (finding no adverse effect in a joint representation of codefendants' case); State v. Brewington, 80 N.C. App. 42, 47–48, 341 N.C. 82, 85–86 (1986) (no showing of actual conflict in a joint representation of codefendants' case); State v. Summerford, 65 N.C. App. 519, 522–24, 309 N.C. 553, 556–57 (1983) (*Cuyler* standard not satisfied in a case where husband and wife were represented by the same counsel, where the wife was less culpable than the husband, and where husband's parents paid lawyer's fees for both defendants); *Willis*, 61 N.C. App. at 248–49, 300 S.E.2d at 832–33 (*Cuyler* test not satisfied where codefendants were represented by the same attorney at sentencing hearing and where defendant argued that conflict prohibited counsel from mentioning defendant's lesser culpability); State v. Howard, 56 N.C. App. 41, 45–47, 286 S.E.2d 853, 857–58 (1982) (*Cuyler* test not satisfied where counsel represented two codefendants).

258. 111 N.C. App. 785, 433 S.E.2d 755 (1993).

259. 111 N.C. App. at 790–91, 433 S.E.2d at 758. During cross-examination of Parker at the defendant's trial, Hatfield acknowledged his dual representation. The court found that once the trial judge is made aware of an attorney's conflict of interest, the "practice should be that the trial judge inquire into an attorney's multiple representation." 111 N.C. App. at 791, 433 S.E.2d at 758. It continued: "No such inquiry was made in the instant case, and the failure of the trial judge to conduct an inquiry, in and of itself, constitutes reversible error." 111 N.C. App. at 792, 433 S.E.2d at 759.

260. 56 N.C. App. 501, 289 S.E.2d 860 (1982).

of stolen goods, a crime also involving the defendant. The defendant alleged in his application for post-conviction relief that Dailey knew that the State sought the defendant's testimony against him but failed to advise the defendant, co-counsel, or the court about the conflict of interest. The court held that the defendant established a conflict of interest by showing that Dailey was under investigation for his own participation in criminal conduct involving the defendant and that Dailey knew about the investigation. The court then concluded that prejudice must be presumed. It went on to hold that because of counsel's ineffectiveness, the defendant's plea was not knowing and voluntary, and it awarded the defendant a new trial.

[3]   Where the Court Knew or Should Have Known about the Conflict

One final procedural context for conflict of interest claims remains to be discussed: when defense counsel did not object to a conflict, but the trial court knew or reasonably should have known about it and did nothing. Until the United States Supreme Court ruled on the applicable test in this context in 2002, a split existed among the lower courts on whether *Holloway* or *Cuyler* governed.

On one side of the lower court split were cases applying *Holloway* and holding that the trial court has a duty to inquire if it knew or should have known about a conflict, regardless of whether the defense raised an objection. These cases held that if the trial court fails to execute its duty to inquire in this context, automatic reversal is required.[261] One 1987 North Carolina Court of Appeals decision indicated that North Carolina fell in this category.[262] More recent North Carolina decisions muddied the water on which rule should apply in this procedural context.[263]

On the other side of the lower court split were cases rejecting application of the

----

261. *See, e.g,* Campbell v. Rice, 265 F.3d 878 (9th Cir. 2001), *abrogated by* Mickens v. Taylor, 122 S. Ct. 1237 (2002), *withdrawn and superseded by* Campbell v. Rice, 302 F.3d 892 (9th Cir. 2002). In Campbell, the prosecutor informed the trial judge that the defendant's counsel was being prosecuted by the same office prosecuting the defendant.

262. *See* State v. Yelton, 87 N.C. App. 554, 557, 361 S.E.2d 753, 755 (1987) ("Once a motion by the State or the defense, or the court on its own motion, raises a possible conflict of interest in a dual representation situation, the trial court must conduct a hearing.").

263. In *State v. Walls*, 342 N.C. 1, 40, 463 S.E.2d 738, 758 (1995), the prosecutor, not the defense counsel, alerted the trial court to a possibility of a conflict of interest between defense counsel and a prosecution witness, whom defense counsel had previously represented. The trial court inquired about the conflict, and defense counsel informed the court that he believed he had made a limited appearance on behalf of the witness and then had no further contact with him. Citing *Cuyler* for the proposition that "[u]nless the trial court knows or reasonably should know that a particular conflict exists, the court need not initiate an inquiry," the court held that the trial court conducted an "adequate inquiry" into the alleged conflict of interest. Thus, the court seems to have applied the *Holloway* rule and implicitly held that no conflict warranting new counsel or a waiver existed. However, the court did not stop there. It went on to apply *Cuyler*'s actual conflict of interest adversely affecting performance test, holding that even if defense counsel actually represented conflicting interests, the defendant failed to show that "the alleged dual representation actually affected the adequacy

Holloway rule in this context and applying *Cuyler* instead. *Mickens v. Taylor,*[264] decided by the United States Court of Appeals for the Fourth Circuit and affirmed by the United States Supreme Court in a decision that resolves the lower court split, fell in this category. In *Mickens,* the defendant was sentenced to death in Virginia state court for the murder of Timothy Hall. At the time of his murder, Hall was the defendant in unrelated criminal charges. After Hall's body was discovered, Judge Aundria Foster dismissed the charges against Hall, noting on the docket sheet that Hall was deceased. Hall's docket sheet indicated that he was represented by attorney Saunders. The defendant was arrested for Hall's murder one day later. Two days after the defendant's arrest, Judge Foster appointed Saunders to represent the defendant in his trial for Hall's murder. The defendant's arrest warrants, which appear to have been before Judge Foster at the time, indicated that Hall was the victim of the crime. Saunders did not raise the conflict of interest with Judge Foster and the judge made no inquiry about it.

While preparing the defendant's federal *habeas corpus* petition, *habeas* counsel inadvertently learned that at the time of Hall's death, Saunders was representing him. Thereafter, the defendant asserted a conflict of interest claim. The federal district court rejected the claim and a divided three-judge panel of the Fourth Circuit reversed. The Fourth Circuit then heard the case en banc and affirmed the district court's denial of the defendant's *habeas* petition.

The en banc panel assumed without deciding that Judge Foster reasonably should have known that the defendant's counsel labored under a potential conflict of interest. The court nevertheless rejected the defendant's argument that *Holloway* required automatic reversal because Judge Foster reasonably should have known of the potential conflict of interest but failed to make the requisite inquiry. Instead, the court held that since no objection was raised before the trial court, the defendant must show that an actual conflict of interest adversely affected Saunders' performance. It went on to hold that the defendant failed to establish adverse effect.

The United States Supreme Court granted *certiorari* and affirmed, resolving the lower court split and holding that *Cuyler* governs in this context. The Court distinguished *Holloway* on grounds that the case before it was not one "in which . . . counsel protested his inability simultaneously to represent multiple defendants."[265] It went on to hold that the trial court's failure to inquire about the potential conflict did not reduce the defendant's burden of proof and that to void his conviction, the defendant must establish "at least . . . that the conflict of interest adversely affected his counsel's

---

of his representation." 342 N.C. at 40–41, 463 S.E.2d at 758. *See also* State v. James, 111 N.C. App. 785, 433 S.E.2d 755 (1993) (holding that the fact that court was made aware of potential conflict but made no inquiry was "in and of itself . . . reversible error"; stating that "[o]rdinarily, we would remand . . . for a hearing to determine if the actual conflict adversely affected . . . performance"; but going on to find, based on the record, that the conflict adversely affected performance and ordering a new trial).

264. 240 F.3d 348 (4th Cir. 2001), *aff'd,* 122 S. Ct. 1237 (2002).

265. Mickens v. Taylor, 122 S. Ct. 1237, 1245 (2002).

performance."[266] Thus, after *Mickens*, it is clear that absent a defense objection on grounds of conflict, *Cuyler* governs even if the trial judge knew or reasonably should have known of the conflict.

§ 1.06 *Harbison* Claims

In the North Carolina state courts, there is one final category of IAC claims that falls outside of the *Strickland* analysis. In *State v. Harbison*,[267] the North Carolina Supreme Court held that when counsel, without the defendant's consent, admits the defendant's guilt to the jury, the defendant is denied effective assistance per se. The defendant in *Harbison* was convicted of second-degree murder and assault with a deadly weapon inflicting serious bodily injury. Throughout the trial, the defendant maintained that he acted in self-defense. His attorney adhered to that defense during his cross-examination of the prosecution's witnesses and during his presentation of the defense. However, during closing argument, counsel stated:

> I have my opinion as to what happened on that April night, and I don't feel that [the defendant] should be found innocent. I think he should do some time to think about what he has done. I think you should find him guilty of manslaughter and not first degree.[268]

The court concluded that this statement constituted an admission of guilt. Citing *Cronic*, it held that "when counsel to the surprise of his client admits his client's guilt, the harm is so likely and so apparent that the issue of prejudice need not be addressed."[269] It concluded: "ineffective assistance of counsel, per se in violation of the Sixth Amendment, has been established in every criminal case in which the defendant's counsel admits the defendant's guilt to the jury without the defendant's consent."[270] Later cases have held that the *Harbison* rule does not apply to sentencing proceedings.[271]

When a defendant asserts a *Harbison* claim, the court first must determine whether counsel made an admission of guilt. Occasionally, counsel will argue that the defendant is innocent of all charges but if found guilty of any, he or she should be found guilty of a lesser crime. Such an argument is not an admission of guilt within the meaning of *Harbison*[272] and must be distinguished from the argument that the defendant

---

266. *Id.*

267. 315 N.C. 175, 337 S.E.2d 504 (1985).

268. 315 N.C. at 177–78, 337 S.E.2d at 506.

269. 315 N.C. at 180, 337 S.E.2d at 507.

270. 315 N.C. at 180, 337 S.E.2d at 507–08.

271. *See* State v. Fletcher, 354 N.C. 455, 481–82, 555 S.E.2d 534, 550 (2001) (capital case), *cert. denied*, 123 S. Ct. 184 (2002); State v. Boyd, 343 N.C. 699, 723, 473 S.E.2d 327, 340 (1996) (capital case); State v. Walls, 342 N.C. 1, 57, 463 S.E.2d 738, 768 (1995) ("*Harbison* applies only to the guilt/innocence phase of a trial.").

272. *See* State v. Gainey, 355 N.C. 73, 558 S.E.2d 463 (2002) (no admission of guilt of

was not innocent and should be convicted of a lesser charge.[273] The key in the former case is that counsel "never conceded that the defendant was guilty of any crime."[274]

If counsel did admit guilt, the court must determine whether the defendant knowingly consented to that admission. If the record includes an express inquiry on this issue by the trial judge, this determination is facilitated.[275] The court will not presume a defendant's lack of consent from a silent record.[276] Thus, where the record is silent, a defendant must offer some proof.

If there was no impermissible admission or if the defendant knowingly consented to the admission, the *Harbison* claim fails. If the IAC claim does not fall within the scope of *Harbison*, it is analyzed under the standard *Strickland* framework.[277]

§ 1.07 Constitutional Right to Counsel Claims and Harmless Error Analysis

The preceding sections set out the appropriate tests for determining whether an IAC claim has merit. Once such a claim has been decided in the defendant's favor on appeal or on a motion for appropriate relief, the decision maker must determine whether the constitutional violation can be considered harmless. The case law is murky on the issue of how and when harmless error analysis applies to IAC claims. The sections that follow explore this difficult area of the law.

[1]   Harmless Error Analysis
[a]   Federal Law Governs

Section 15A-1443 of the North Carolina General Statutes (hereinafter G.S.) is in the article of the North Carolina Criminal Procedure Act pertaining to appeals

---

murder where counsel stated: "[I]f he's guilty of anything, he's guilty of accessory after the fact. He's guilty of possession of a stolen vehicle."), *cert. denied*, 123 S. Ct. 182 (2002); State v. Harvell, 334 N.C. 356, 361, 432 S.E.2d 125, 128 (1993).

273. *See supra* p. 48 (discussing *Harbison*, which involved such an argument).

274. *See Harvell*, 334 N.C. at 361, 432 S.E.2d at 128.

275. In *State v. House*, 340 N.C. 187, 197, 456 S.E.2d 292, 297 (1995), the North Carolina Supreme Court "urged both the bar and the trial bench to be diligent in making a full record of a defendant's consent when a *Harbison* issue arises at trial."

276. *See Boyd*, 343 N.C. at 722, 473 S.E.2d at 339 ("This Court will not presume defendant's lack of consent from a silent record."); *House*, 340 N.C. at 196, 456 S.E.2d at 297.

277. *See* State v. Fletcher, 354 N.C. 455, 482, 555 S.E.2d 534, 550 (2001) ("[H]aving determined that the alleged concession did not constitute ineffective assistance of counsel *per se*, we proceed to analyze counsel's actions under a traditional *Strickland* analysis."), *cert. denied*, 123 S. Ct. 184 (2002); State v. Fisher, 318 N.C. 512, 533, 350 S.E.2d 334, 346 (1986) ("As this case does not fall with the *Harbison* line of cases where violation of the defendant's Sixth Amendment rights are presumed, the defendant's claim of [IAC] must be analyzed using the *Strickland* factors"); State v. McDowell, 329 N.C. 363, 387, 407 S.E.2d 200, 213 (1991) (only "where a knowing consent has been demonstrated, . . . [should] the issue concerning [IAC] be . . . examined pursuant to the normal set forth in *Strickland v. Washington*.").

to the appellate division. Subsection (b) provides that when an error involves a violation of the defendant's rights under the United States Constitution, it is deemed prejudicial unless the State can establish that the error is harmless beyond a reasonable doubt. This standard has been incorporated into the statutory provisions governing motions for appropriate relief.[278] All IAC claims asserted under the federal Constitution involve an alleged violation of federal constitutional rights.[279] Thus, at first blush, it appears that G.S. 15A-1443(b) governs all such claims when raised in motions for appropriate relief or on direct appeal. This view, however, is erroneous.

Federal law, not G.S. 15A-1443(b), governs review of federal constitutional violations. As the United States Supreme Court made clear in its seminal harmless error case, *Chapman v. California*,[280] when a federal constitutional right is at issue, federal law, not a state harmless error rule, applies.[281] Thus, when a defendant asserts and establishes that IAC resulted in a violation of federal constitutional rights, federal harmless error law, not case law interpreting G.S. 15A-1443(b), governs. The North Carolina courts have recognized this principle.[282]

[b]   The Federal Standard

The United States Supreme Court's seminal decision on harmless error is *Chapman v. California*.[283] *Chapman* rejected the contention that the federal Constitution required automatic reversal for all constitutional errors. Instead, it held that constitutional errors should be evaluated against a harmless error standard. Under that standard, the error will require reversal unless the court is convinced "beyond a reasonable doubt" that it was harmless. An error is harmless if it "did not contribute to the verdict obtained."[284] The *Chapman* harmless error rule is designed to avoid "setting aside convictions for small errors or defects that have little, if any, likelihood of having changed the result of the trial"[285] and to "promote[] public respect for the criminal process by focusing

---

278. *See* G.S. 15A-1420(c)(6).

279. *See supra* pp. 1–2 (discussing the constitutional bases of IAC claims).

280. 386 U.S. 18 (1967).

281. *See id.* at 20–21.

282. *See* State v. Huff, 325 N.C. 1, 34, 381 S.E.2d 635, 654 (1989) (recognizing that "the General Assembly has no authority to fix the standard for reversal in review of violations of the federal Constitution"), *vacated on other grounds*, 497 U.S. 1021 (1990); State v. Colbert, 311 N.C. 283, 286, 316 S.E.2d 79, 81 (1984) ("in federal constitutional issues . . . the standards of the United States Supreme Court apply in determining harmless error [not G.S. § 15A-1443(b)]"); State v. May, 110 N.C. App. 268, 270, 429 S.E.2d 360, 362 (1993) ("[W]hether a defendant's conviction for a crime will withstand his denial of rights guaranteed by the Federal Constitution is a question that must be answered by reference to federal law.").

283. 386 U.S. 18 (1967).

284. *Id.* at 24. This section continues with a discussion on *Chapman*'s applicability to Sixth Amendment IAC claims. For a detailed discussion on the substance of the *Chapman* inquiry as applied to constitutional errors generally, see LaFave, *supra* note 2, § 27.6(e).

285. *Chapman*, 386 U.S. at 22.

on the underlying fairness of the trial rather than on the virtually inevitable presence of immaterial error."[286]

Over the years, the United States Supreme Court has applied the *Chapman* standard to a wide range of constitutional errors.[287] However, the Court also has held that a number of errors are not subject to harmless error inquiry and instead require automatic reversal.[288] These errors, however, "are the exception and not the rule."[289]

In *Arizona v. Fulminante*,[290] the Court clarified that only errors involving a "structural defect affecting the framework within which the trial proceeds, rather than simply an error in the trial process itself" fall outside of the *Chapman* harmless error rule and warrant automatic reversal.[291] The sections below explore the application of the *Chapman* harmless error standard and the *Fulminante* "structural defects" exception to violations of the Sixth Amendment right to effective assistance of counsel.

[2]   The Relationship between Harmless Error Analysis and Ineffective Assistance Claims

The law relating to harmless error analysis and IAC claims is far from clear. Until the Supreme Court clarifies the law, decision makers are likely to be confronted with a host of arguments regarding why harmless error analysis applies or does not apply to a particular IAC claim. The sections that follow attempt to lay out the various and sometimes overlapping arguments that may be asserted in this difficult area of the law.

[a]   Structural Defects
[i]   Denial of Counsel Cases

It may be argued that denial of counsel violations are structural defects and therefore not subject to harmless error review. A proponent of such an argument would likely rely on the United States Supreme Court cases recognizing that denial of the

---

286. Rose v. Clark, 478 U.S. 570, 577 (1986) (quotation omitted).

287. *See id.* at 576–82 (holding that harmless error analysis applies to erroneous malice instruction in murder case that impermissibly shifted the burden of proof; collecting cases applying *Chapman* to other errors); LaFave, *supra* note 2, § 27.6(d), at 948–49 (collecting cases). In *Chapman*, the Court applied the standard to the prosecution's comment and the trial judge's jury instruction on defendant's failure to testify. *See Chapman*, 386 U.S. at 24–26 (finding that State failed to demonstrate beyond a reasonable doubt that the prosecutor's comments and the jury instruction "did not contribute to [defendants'] convictions").

288. *Chapman* expressly recognized that some constitutional rights are "so basic to a fair trial that their infraction can never be treated as harmless error" and cited several cases applying this rule. *Chapman*, 386 U.S. at 23 & n.8 (citing Payne v. Arkansas, 356 U.S. 560 (1958) (coerced confession); Gideon v. Wainwright, 372 U.S. 335 (1963) (right to counsel); Tumey v. Ohio, 273 U.S. 510 (1927) (impartial judge)). *But see* Arizona v. Fulminante, 499 U.S. 279 (1991) (applying harmless error analysis to coerced confession).

289. *Rose*, 478 U.S. at 578; *see also Arizona*, 499 U.S. at 306 ("most constitutional errors can be harmless") (Rehnquist, J.).

290. 499 U.S. 279 (1991).

291. *Id.* at 310 (applying harmless error analysis to coerced confession).

right to counsel is a "structural defect[] in the constitution of the trial mechanism, which def[ies] analysis by 'harmless error' standards" and "requires automatic reversal of the conviction because [it] infect[s] the entire trial process."[292] In fact, in *Fulminante* itself, the Court noted that denial of counsel was such an error.[293]

However, not all denials of counsel constitute structural errors warranting an exception from the *Chapman* harmless error rule. In *Coleman v. Alabama*,[294] for example, the Court found that the defendant was denied counsel at a critical stage in the proceeding—the preliminary hearing—in violation of his Sixth Amendment right. In spite of this, the Court remanded the case for a harmless error analysis under *Chapman*, expressly stating that the test to be applied on remand was "whether the denial of counsel at the preliminary hearing was harmless error under *Chapman v. California*."[295] The Court took the same approach in *Satterwhite v. Texas*.[296] There, the trial court admitted evidence obtained in violation of the capital defendant's Sixth Amendment right to consult with counsel before submitting to psychiatric examinations designed to determine his future dangerousness. The United States Supreme Court held that the Sixth Amendment violation was subject to harmless error analysis.[297]

---

292. Brecht v. Abrahamson, 507 U.S. 619, 629–30 (1993) (*Doyle* error is susceptible to harmless error analysis) (quotation omitted). Even before the structural defect standard became part of the Court's analysis, it refused to require a showing of prejudice where a denial of counsel occurred at a critical stage. *See* Hamilton v. Alabama, 368 U.S. 52, 55 (1961) ("When one pleads to a capital charge without benefit of counsel, we do not stop to determine whether prejudice resulted.").

293. *Fulminante*, 499 U.S. at 309–10 (citing *Gideon*, a right to counsel case). Pre-*Fulminante* cases are in accord. In *Holloway v. Arkansas*, 435 U.S. 475 (1978), the Court stated:

> [T]his Court has concluded that the assistance of counsel is among those constitutional rights so basic to a fair trial that their infraction can never be treated as harmless error. Accordingly, when a defendant is deprived of the presence or assistance of his attorney, either throughout the prosecution or during a critical stage in, at least, the prosecution of a capital offense, reversal is automatic.

Id. at 489 (citation and quotation omitted).

The Court's treatment of denial of counsel cases as involving structural errors is consistent with the presumption of prejudice that applies to such violations. *See supra* p. 22.

294. 399 U.S. 1 (1970)

295. *Id.* at 11.

296. 486 U.S. 249 (1988).

297. *See id.* at 258 (going on to hold that the error was not harmless beyond a reasonable doubt). In *Brooks v. Tennessee*, 406 U.S. 605 (1972), the United States Supreme Court held that the defendant's right to the "guiding hand of counsel" is violated when the defendant and counsel are "restricted in deciding whether, and when in the course of presenting his defense, the accused should take the stand." *Id.* at 613. Although the court ordered a new trial, its opinion indicates it might have been willing to undertake harmless error analysis, had the issue been argued by the State. *See id.* at 613 ("The state makes no claim that this was harmless error.").

The Court has indicated that the distinction between denial of counsel cases subject to harmless error review and denial of counsel cases constituting structural defects and warranting automatic reversal is whether "the deprivation of the right to counsel affected—and contaminated—the entire criminal proceeding."[298] Among the cases where the deprivation was found to "pervade the entire proceeding"[299] are those where defense counsel labored under a conflict of interest throughout the entire proceeding, those where the defendant was denied counsel throughout the entire proceeding, and those where counsel's absence from the arraignment affected the entire trial because defenses not asserted at arraignment were irretrievably lost.[300] Among the denial of counsel cases where the violation was subjected to harmless error review are cases like *Satterwhite*, where the effect of the Sixth Amendment violation is limited to the erroneous admission of evidence at trial,[301] and *Coleman v. Alabama*, where, apparently, the Sixth Amendment violation did not pervade the entire proceeding.[302]

Where the line should be drawn between these groups of cases is not clear. After all, a denial of counsel only can occur when the proceeding at which counsel was denied is deemed critical. The determination of whether a proceeding is critical turns on "whether potential substantial prejudice to the defendant's rights inheres in the . . . confrontation

---

298. *Satterwhite*, 486 U.S. at 257.

299. *Id.* at 256.

300. *See id.* (citing cases).

301. *See id.* at 257 (citing cases).

302. 399 U.S. 1 (1970). *Coleman* held that the denial of counsel did not pervade the entire proceeding and that thus the claim was subject to harmless error review. This holding is difficult to reconcile with the Court's rationale for holding that a preliminary hearing is a critical stage in the proceeding. *Coleman* held that "the guiding hand of counsel at the preliminary hearing is essential to protect the indigent accused against an erroneous or improper prosecution." *Id.* at 9. It explained:

> First, the lawyer's skilled examination and cross-examination of witnesses may expose fatal weaknesses in the State's case that may lead the magistrate to refuse to bind the accused over. Second, in any event, the skilled interrogation of witnesses by an experienced lawyer can fashion a vital impeachment tool for use in cross-examination of the State's witnesses at the trial, or preserve testimony favorable to the accused of a witness who does not appear at the trial. Third, trained counsel can more effectively discover the case the State has against his client and make possible the preparation of a proper defense to meet that case at the trial. Fourth, counsel can also be influential at the preliminary hearing in making effective arguments for the accused on such matters as the necessity for an early psychiatric examination or bail.
>
> The inability of the indigent accused on his own to realize these advantages of a lawyer's assistance compels the conclusion that the Alabama preliminary hearing is a "critical stage" of the State's criminal process at which the accused is "as much entitled to such aid (of counsel) as at the trial itself."

Id. at 9–10 (quoting Powell v. Alabama, 287 U.S. 45, 57 (1932)). This reasoning also supports the view that a denial of counsel at a preliminary hearing is a violation that contaminates the whole proceeding. Notwithstanding this, *Coleman* subjected the violation to harmless error review.

and the ability of counsel to help avoid the prejudice."[303] Thus, the Court's analysis requires the decision maker to distinguish between cases where the denial of counsel satisfies that standard and cases where the potential substantial prejudice was so great as to contaminate the entire proceeding.[304]

[ii] Attorney Error Cases

It may be argued that attorney error claims are structural defects warranting automatic reversal. Such a view finds support in *State v. May*.[305] In *May*, the North Carolina Court of Appeals held that unconstitutional attorney error in connection with a guilty plea cannot be subjected to the *Chapman* inquiry. The court held that because there was no trial, it was not possible to engage in the harmless error inquiry. It stated:

> [T]he trial court found that . . . [IAC] led to [defendant's] decision to enter guilty pleas. It made this finding after holding extensive hearings in order to rule on defendant's motion for appropriate relief. In so doing, the court had a preview of the evidence that would have been presented at trial and, in light of such evidence, made its determination that counsel's ineffective assistance was harmless beyond a reasonable doubt. As thorough as the hearings may have been they were no substitute for a trial by jury.[306]

Additionally, *Rose v. Lee*,[307] decided by the United States Court of Appeals for the Fourth Circuit, can be read as suggesting that the Fourth Circuit views certain attorney error claims as structural errors that are not subject to harmless error analysis. In *Rose*, the defendant contended that his attorneys rendered ineffective assistance at his capital sentencing proceeding by failing to adequately investigate and produce significant mitigating evidence regarding his mental health. Although the Fourth Circuit found no ineffectiveness under *Strickland*, it indicated that "[o]f course . . . if [the defendant] was denied effective assistance of counsel, the error would not be subject to harmless error review."[308]

Notwithstanding *May* and *Rose*, it is difficult to argue that *all* Sixth Amendment violations involving attorney error automatically fall outside of the scope of *Chapman* harmless error analysis because all such violations are structural errors. The United States Supreme Court has indicated that the distinction between denial of counsel violations

---

303. *Id.* at 9 (quotation omitted).

304. The North Carolina Supreme Court has not expressly explored this distinction and its cases are not consistent on the issue. *Compare* State v. Colbert, 311 N.C. 283, 316 S.E.2d 79 (1984) (holding that the trial court violated the defendant's right to counsel by beginning jury selection in counsel's absence and concluding that the error could not be treated as harmless) *with* State v. Maher, 305 N.C. 544, 550, 290 S.E.2d 694, 697–98 (1982) (holding that defendant was denied his right to effective assistance where counsel was not afforded adequate time to prepare and stating that the denial was subject to harmless error analysis).

305. 110 N.C. App. 268, 429 S.E.2d 360 (1993).

306. 110 N.C. App. at 271, 429 S.E.2d at 363 (discussing *Arizona*).

307. 252 F.3d 676 (4th Cir.), *cert. denied*, 122 S. Ct. 318 (2001).

308. *Id.* at 689 (citing Williams v. Taylor, 529 U.S. 362, 375 (2000), as "reiterating the well-settled rule that '[t]he deprivation of the right to the effective assistance of counsel' is a structural error to which harmless error review does not apply.").

subject to harmless error review and those constituting structural defects warranting automatic reversal is whether the violation affected and contaminated the entire proceeding.[309] Given this and the broad language of the Court's decision in *Arizona*, it is difficult to say that all attorney error IAC violations are structural errors warranting automatic reversal.

[b]   Claims Where Defendant Must Prove Prejudice

One commentator has suggested that the *Chapman* harmless error analysis has no relevance to errors that are "harmful by definition." According to this view, "it would be wasted effort to look to *Chapman* where the constitutional violation is one . . . that already requires—as an element of the violation—a finding of likely prejudicial impact."[310] The two-pronged *Strickland* test applies to the great majority of IAC claims.[311] Under that test, a defendant must establish deficient performance and prejudice.[312] Thus, claims analyzed under *Strickland* require a finding of prejudice. Applying the view stated above, if a defendant establishes prejudice under *Strickland*'s second prong, it makes no sense to engage in harmless error analysis; the prosecution cannot prove that the error is harmless beyond a reasonable doubt if the defendant has already established that the error is prejudicial.

There is no United States Supreme Court case law directly on this point, and the Court has made statements that cut both ways on this issue.[313] Its most recent statement, however, supports the notion that harmless error analysis is unnecessary once the defendant has established prejudice under the *Strickland* analysis.[314] The federal circuit courts have either expressly or impliedly declined to engage in harmless error analysis once the defendant satisfies *Strickland*'s second prong.[315] Thus, there appear to be two arguments that harmless error analysis has no application to attorney error IAC

---

309. *See supra* p. 53.

310. *See* LaFave, *supra* note 2, § 27.6(d), at 947.

311. *See supra* note 89 and accompanying text.

312. *See id.*

313. *Compare* Lockhart v. Fretwell, 506 U.S. 364, 369 n.2 (1993) (addressing an IAC claim and suggesting such a claim is susceptible to harmless error inquiry: "[H]armless error analysis is triggered only *after* the reviewing court discovers that an error has been committed. . . . Since we find no constitutional error, we need not . . . consider harmlessness.") *with* Kyles v. Whitley, 514 U.S. 419, 435–36 & n.9 (1995) ("once there has been a *Bagley* error . . . , it cannot subsequently be found harmless" under *Kotteakos*) (citing Hill v. Lockhart, 28 F.3d 832, 839 (8th Cir. 1994), as stating: "it is unnecessary to add a separate layer of harmless-error analysis to an evaluation of whether a petitioner . . . has presented a constitutionally significant claim of [IAC]").

314. *See Kyles*, 514 U.S. at 435–36 & n.9.

315. *See, e.g.,* Hill v. Lockhart, 28 F.3d. 832, 838 (8th Cir. 1994) (addressing prejudice under *Strickland* and harmless error under *Kotteakos* and holding: "Absent more explicit direction from the Supreme Court . . . we hold that it is unnecessary to add a separate layer of harmless-error analysis to an evaluation of whether a petitioner in a habeas case has presented a constitutionally significant claim for [IAC]."); Baylor v. Estelle, 94 F.3d 1321, 1324–25 (9th Cir. 1996) (finding that defendant established both prongs of the *Strickland* analysis, not expressly mentioning harmless error analysis, and not going on to engage in that analysis).

claims: (1) such claims are structural errors falling outside of the harmless error rule;[316] and (2) because the defendant has already established prejudice, harmless error analysis has no relevance.

[c] Claims Where Prejudice Is Presumed

In several types of IAC claims, defendants are relieved of the burden of showing actual prejudice and prejudice is presumed. Included in this group are:

- cases like *Roe* where counsel's deficient performance deprived a defendant of a proceeding which he or she wanted and had a right to[317]
- denial of counsel cases
- conflict of interest cases where there is a *Holloway* violation[318] or where the *Cuyler* test is satisfied[319]
- *Harbison* claims

In all of these situations, prejudice is presumed. It may be argued that to apply harmless error analysis where prejudice has been presumed makes no sense because it would vitiate the presumption. In fact, in some of these cases, the courts have declined to engage in harmless error analysis, either expressly[320] or impliedly.[321] On the other hand, there is a difficulty with the broad assertion that harmless error has no applicability where a presumption of prejudice applies. In one of the categories of claims where that presumption applies—denial of counsel claims—the United States Supreme Court has expressly rejected the argument that harmless error can have no application. As discussed above, the Court has held that only those denials of counsel that constitute structural errors warrant automatic reversal. This suggests that the nature of the error (structural versus nonstructural)—not the presumption of prejudice—is the key to determining whether harmless error applies.

---

316. *See supra* pp. 54–55.

317. *See supra* pp. 20–21.

318. *See supra* pp. 35–39.

319. *See supra* pp. 39–48.

320. *See* Holloway v. Arkansas, 435 U.S. 475, 491 (1978) ("[T]o assess the impact of a conflict of interests on the attorney's options, tactics, and decisions in plea negotiations would be virtually impossible. Thus, an inquiry into a claim of harmless error here would require, unlike most cases, unguided speculation."); Cuyler v. Sullivan, 446 U.S. 335, 349 (1980) ("*Glasser* established that unconstitutional multiple representation is never harmless error."); *see also* State v. Howard, 56 N.C. App. 41, 46, 286 S.E.2d 853, 857 (1982) ("Unconstitutional multiple representation is never harmless error. . . .").

321. *See, e.g.,* Roe v. Flores-Ortega, 528 U.S. 470 (2000) (remanding for further proceedings consistent with an opinion that did not mention harmless error analysis); State v. James, 111 N.C. App. 785, 788–92, 433 S.E.2d 755, 757–59 (1993) (finding the *Cuyler* standard satisfied and not going on to engage in a harmless error analysis before ordering a new trial). *See also infra* p. 57 (discussing *Harbison* claims).

[d] Harmless Error and *Harbison* Claims

In *State v. Harbison*,[322] the North Carolina Supreme Court held that a defendant is denied effective assistance when defense counsel, without the defendant's consent, admits the defendant's guilt to the jury.[323] In this context, counsel is per se ineffective and no showing of prejudice is required. In *Harbison*, the court found that such an admission had occurred and remanded for a new trial. No mention of harmless error was made. Thus, *Harbison* suggests that in North Carolina, harmless error analysis does not apply once the court has found per se ineffectiveness because of an unconsented-to admission of guilt.

---

322. 315 N.C. 175, 337 S.E.2d 504 (1985).

323. *See supra* pp. 48–49 (discussing *Harbison* in more detail).

Part II: Catalogue of North Carolina Ineffective Assistance of Counsel Cases

This part presents a catalogue of published North Carolina appellate cases addressing IAC claims.[1] The catalogue is divided into categories of specific allegations of ineffectiveness, arranged to roughly track the order of a criminal trial. It begins with cases in which the defendant alleged ineffectiveness in the pretrial stages of a criminal case and moves on to cases in which the defendant alleged ineffectiveness at trial and on appeal. Since defendants asserting IAC often assert more than one such claim, a number of cases are listed in more than one category. In each category, successful IAC claims are presented first.[2]

§ 2.01 Claims of Ineffectiveness at the Pretrial Stage

[1]   Failure to Move for a Bill of Particulars

State v. Swann, 322 N.C. 666, 684, 370 S.E.2d 533, 543 (1988) (counsel was not ineffective by failing to move for a bill of particulars that would have disclosed the time of day that the offenses allegedly occurred, the exact location where they allegedly occurred, and the exact conduct at issue; knowing this information would not have helped defendant develop an alibi defense since he did not know where he was on those days and he had adequate information without the bill of particulars to determine whether there were witnesses or physical evidence).

---

1. The catalogue includes criminal cases decided after the North Carolina Supreme Court's decision in *State v. Braswell*, 312 N.C. 553, 324 S.E.2d 241 (1985). In *Braswell*, the North Carolina Supreme Court adopted the federal IAC standard, as set forth in *Strickland v. Washington*, 466 U.S. 668 (1984), for IAC claims alleging that attorney error resulted in a violation of state constitutional rights.

2. Many of the cases listed in the catalogue are attorney error cases decided under the *Strickland* test. Where this is the case, the phrase "counsel was not ineffective" is used to indicate that the defendant's claim was rejected on grounds that counsel's performance was not deficient and/or that no prejudice resulted.

[2]   Failure to Move to Require Election between Charges

State v. Swann, 322 N.C. 666, 684, 370 S.E.2d 533, 543 (1988) (counsel was not ineffective by failing to move to require the State to elect between the charges of first-degree sexual offense and taking indecent liberties with a child where election was not required).

[3]   Pretrial Discovery and *Brady* Issues

State v. Williams, 350 N.C. 1, 18–19, 510 S.E.2d 626, 638 (1999) (counsel in a capital case was not ineffective by failing to object to the prosecutor's alleged misrepresentation of a pretrial order that resulted in counsel turning over a psychiatrist's report where the State was entitled to the report).

State v. Heatwole, 344 N.C. 1, 13–14, 473 S.E.2d 310, 315–16 (1996) (State's alleged *Brady* violation did not render capital defendant's counsel ineffective; even assuming that the State attempted to suppress evidence, defendant could not show prejudice).

State v. Swann, 322 N.C. 666, 683–85, 370 S.E.2d 533, 543–44 (1988) (counsel was not ineffective by failing to move to compel discovery where counsel was given some items at trial and defendant provided no indication of what else could have been discovered with the motion; counsel was not ineffective by failing to make a *Brady* motion to obtain information regarding the victim's mental condition where defendant was in a position to know that information and there was no indication that the State had any more detailed information than defendant; counsel was not ineffective by failing to make a *Brady* motion to obtain a transcript of an interview of the victim by a third person where the district attorney gave a transcript of his interview of the victim to defendant's counsel before trial and counsel was aware that the victim had been equivocal in interviews; counsel was not ineffective by failing to make a *Brady* motion to obtain prior criminal records of the State's witnesses where these records are not discoverable under *Brady*).

State v. Lowery, 318 N.C. 54, 68, 347 S.E.2d 729, 739 (1986) (counsel was not ineffective by failing to make a *Brady* motion requesting disclosure of statements made by the victim's children; defendant's request for voluntary discovery contained a *Brady* request and nothing in the record indicated that counsel was not apprised of the children's statements).

State v. Johnson, 124 N.C. App. 462, 469, 478 S.E.2d 16, 21 (1996) (defendant was not denied effective assistance when his attorney withdrew a motion to compel disclosure of an informant's identity; because defendant was acquitted of the charge to which the informant's testimony related, no prejudice resulted).

[4]   Failure to Assert a Speedy Trial Violation

State v. Grooms, 353 N.C. 50, 64–65, 540 S.E.2d 713, 722–23 (2000) (counsel was not ineffective in failing to assert capital defendant's right to a speedy trial where defendant's right to a speedy trial was not violated and he was not entitled to dismissal of the charges), *cert. denied*, 122 S. Ct. 93 (2001).

State v. Johnson, 124 N.C. App. 462, 465–68, 478 S.E.2d 16, 18–21 (1996) (counsel was not ineffective by failing to move to dismiss because of a speedy trial violation where defendant was not denied his right to a speedy trial and thus the result of the proceeding would not have been different if counsel had made the motion).

[5]   Entering into a Stipulation

State v. Aiken, 73 N.C. App. 487, 492, 326 S.E.2d 919, 922 (1985) (counsel was not ineffective in a rape case by entering into a stipulation admitting into evidence the results of the victim's vaginal examination where the defense was based on consent and thus test results indicating that the victim had sexual intercourse were not prejudicial to defendant).

State v. Cogdell, 74 N.C. App. 647, 652, 329 S.E.2d 675, 678 (1985) (counsel was not ineffective by stipulating that the bullet wound inflicted serious injury when doctor's report indicated that bullet caused "very serious injury" and "significant damage [which] could easily have proven fatal").

[6]   Failure to Make a Motion *in Limine*

State v. Swann, 322 N.C. 666, 686–87, 370 S.E.2d 533, 544–45 (1988) (counsel was not ineffective by failing to file motions *in limine* to exclude certain testimony where some of the testimony would not have been excluded and IAC could not be established on the grounds asserted; no prejudice resulted from counsel's failure because a ruling on a motion *in limine* is interlocutory and might have changed at trial; failure to make the motions did not prevent defendant from later objecting to the evidence at trial; defendant did not demonstrate prejudice by the admission of any of the evidence for which he claimed a motion *in limine* should have been made).

State v. Blackwell, 133 N.C. App. 31, 37–38, 514 S.E.2d 116, 120–21 (1999) (counsel was not ineffective by failing to make motions in limine; "[a]lthough it may have been prudent" to have filed the motions, counsel made the appropriate arguments in court).

[7]   Failure to Move for a Change of Venue

State v. Lowery, 318 N.C. 54, 68, 347 S.E.2d 729, 739 (1986) (counsel was not ineffective by failing to join in codefendant's motion for change of venue where that motion was denied and where defendant presented no evidence suggesting that he did not receive a fair trial in the jurisdiction).

[8]   Ineffectiveness in Connection with a Motion to Suppress Evidence

State v. Grooms, 353 N.C. 50, 73–75, 540 S.E.2d 713, 727–29 (2000) (counsel was not ineffective by failing to object to the State's use of a search warrant instead of a nontestimonial identification order to obtain samples of defendant's blood, hair, and saliva; because the State properly obtained the search warrant and defendant had no right to presence of counsel at its execution, defendant could not show that counsel's performance was deficient or that prejudice resulted), *cert. denied*, 122 S. Ct. 93 (2001).

State v. Pittman, 332 N.C. 244, 261, 420 S.E.2d 437, 447 (1992) (rejecting defendant's contention that the trial court violated his right to effective assistance by refusing to hear his counsel's arguments in favor of his motion to suppress; defense counsel never made any effort to make argument in support of the motion and only indicated to the court that he had three cases discussing the State's burden on the motion, which the court declined to review).

State v. China, 150 N.C. App. 469, 564 S.E.2d 64, 71 (2002) (rejecting defendant's claim that counsel was ineffective by failing to move to suppress evidence obtained after entry into defendant's home; warrantless entry did not violate the Fourth Amendment and evidence was in plain view).

State v. Frazier, 142 N.C. App. 361, 367–70, 542 S.E.2d 682, 687–89 (2001) (counsel was not ineffective by failing to move to suppress evidence and statement made by defendant before trial where the evidence and statement were admissible).

State v. Bailey, 145 N.C. App. 13, 23–24, 548 S.E.2d 814, 821 (2001) (rejecting defendant's argument that counsel was ineffective by moving to suppress defendant's written statement to one detective and not moving to suppress his similar oral statement to another officer; even if counsel erred, no prejudice resulted where evidence establishing that defendant confessed would have been admitted through other sources).

State v. Aiken, 73 N.C. App. 487, 492–93, 326 S.E.2d 919, 922–23 (1985) (counsel was not ineffective by failing to seek suppression of defendant's statement to the police, a strategy defendant contended was his sole defense; the defense presented at trial was consent and it would have been frivolous for counsel to move to suppress a voluntary statement that was consistent with this defense; also, there did not appear to be any basis upon which the statement could have been suppressed).

[9]   Failure to Move to Disqualify Witnesses

State v. Swann, 322 N.C. 666, 686, 370 S.E.2d 533, 544 (1988) (counsel was not ineffective by failing to move to disqualify a witness on grounds of incompetence where the record revealed that the witness was competent).

[10]   Failure to Move for or Obtain Severance

State v. Stroud, 147 N.C. App. 549, 557 S.E.2d 544 (2001) (on direct appeal finding that defendant had "prematurely asserted" a claim that counsel was ineffective by not moving to sever; dismissing without prejudice to defendant's right to assert the claim in a motion for appropriate relief).

State v. Beckham, 145 N.C. App. 119, 124–26, 550 S.E.2d 231, 236 (2001) (rejecting defendant's claim that counsel was ineffective by failing to move for a severance of rape and indecent liberties charges where the offenses were not sufficiently separate and distinct circumstantially to render their consolidation prejudicial).

State v. Summers, 92 N.C. App. 453, 458–60, 374 S.E.2d 631, 635 (1988) (rejecting defendant's argument that counsel was ineffective by failing to move for severance of rape and indecent liberties charges where reason asserted for need for severance was invalid).

[11]   Failure to Move for Blood Testing

State v. Aiken, 73 N.C. App. 487, 492, 326 S.E.2d 919, 922 (1985) (counsel in a rape case was not ineffective by failing to move for blood type testing of sperm found in victim's vagina where defendant's defense was consent).

[12]   Competency Hearings and Psychiatric Examinations

State v. Beckham, 145 N.C. App. 119, 126, 550 S.E.2d 231, 236 (2001) (rejecting defendant's claim that counsel was ineffective by failing to demand a hearing on defendant's competency where there was insufficient evidence of incompetency and defendant failed to show that counsel was deficient).

State v. Jackson, 77 N.C. App. 491, 499–500, 335 S.E.2d 903, 908–09 (1985) (court-ordered psychiatric examination that dealt with defendant's sanity at the time of the offenses did not violate his right to effective assistance; when trial judge ordered the examination, counsel was present, had an opportunity to be heard, and had actual notice of the examination's scope; defendant elected to pursue an insanity defense, with notice the psychiatrist might be offered in rebuttal; such a defendant may be ordered to undergo examination, and there is no right to counsel at the time of the examination), *called into doubt on other grounds* by State v. Huff, 325 N.C. 1, 381 S.E.2d 635 (1989), *vacated on other grounds by* 497 U.S. 1021 (1990).

[13]   Failure to Make Any Pretrial Motions

State v. Edwards, 73 N.C. App. 599, 602, 327 S.E.2d 16, 18 (1985) (counsel was not ineffective by failing to make any pretrial motions; such a failure is not ineffectiveness per se; the record reflected that counsel was prepared to and did capably conduct the defense, including vigorously examining witnesses, using information apparently discovered in the preliminary proceedings, timely requesting *voir dire* hearings, obtaining suppression of incriminating evidence, and presenting evidence on defendant's behalf).

[14]   Inadequate Pretrial Preparation

State v. Swann, 322 N.C. 666, 681–83, 370 S.E.2d 533, 541–42 (1988) (counsel was not ineffective by failing to properly investigate the case and prepare for trial; specifically, counsel was not ineffective by failing to (1) interview twenty-one potential witnesses before trial, twelve of whom testified at trial, where testimony of those who did not testify would have been cumulative and would not have changed the result of the trial; (2) visit the crime scene or have photographs made of it where such pictorial evidence would have been cumulative; (3) have a chemical analysis performed on the mattress on which the alleged incident occurred when defendant never had such an analysis performed and thus could not show that the result of the trial would have been different had it been done; and (4) discover that the victim's mother had a motive for prosecuting defendant where defendant testified at the hearing that counsel asked him why the victim's mother would prosecute him and he did not tell counsel of the alleged motive at that time).

State v. Broome, 136 N.C. App. 82, 92, 523 S.E.2d 448, 455–56 (1999) (rejecting defendant's argument that counsel's lack of knowledge about an informant's plea agreement constituted ineffective assistance where court was not persuaded that the outcome of the trial was affected by counsel's alleged failing), *review denied*, 351 N.C. 362, 543 S.E.2d 136 (2000).

State v. Howie, 116 N.C. App. 609, 614–15, 448 S.E.2d 867, 870 (1994) (declining to address the details of defendant's contention that counsel inadequately prepared for trial where there was overwhelming evidence of guilt and no possibility that the jury would have reached a different verdict but for counsel's alleged errors).

State v. Attmore, 92 N.C. App. 385, 391–94, 374 S.E.2d 649, 654–55 (1988) (counsel was not ineffective by failing to investigate an insanity defense; although "counsel deserves no commendation for his pretrial preparation," he had no duty to explore an insanity defense where defendant offered nothing to put him on notice that the defense might be available and where even if the insanity defense had been proffered, the result of the trial would have been the same).

State v. Blackwell, 133 N.C. App. 31, 37–38, 514 S.E.2d 116, 120–21 (1999) (counsel was not ineffective by failing to properly investigate defendant's prior crimes when given notice of them; the court did not specifically address this allegation but concluded that counsel "vigorously and competently examined all the witnesses" and his performance did not fall below an objective standard of reasonableness).

[15] Failure to Include Witness on a Pretrial Witness List or Failure to Subpoena, Interview, or Prepare a Witness

State v. Gary, 348 N.C. 510, 514–16, 501 S.E.2d 57, 61–62 (1998) (counsel was not ineffective by failing to issue process for or call an alibi witness; appointment of substitute counsel was not required where defendant and counsel disagreed over the tactical decision of whether the witness would be helpful).

State v. Swann, 322 N.C. 666, 681, 370 S.E.2d 533, 541–42 (1988) (counsel was not ineffective by failing to interview twenty-one potential witnesses before trial, twelve of whom testified at trial, where the witnesses whom counsel failed to interview would have offered only cumulative testimony).

State v. Miller, 142 N.C. App. 435, 445, 543 S.E.2d 201, 207–08 (2001) (counsel was not ineffective by failing to include on the pretrial witness list a witness likely to commit perjury; counsel's decision was professionally reasonable).

State v. Blackwell, 133 N.C. App. 31, 37–38, 514 S.E.2d 116, 120–21 (1999) (counsel was not ineffective by failing to file subpoenas; the court did not specifically address this allegation but concluded that counsel's performance did not fall below an objective standard of reasonableness).

State v. Braswell, 312 N.C. 553, 565–66, 324 S.E.2d 241, 249–50 (1985) (counsel was not ineffective by failing to properly interview a defense witness before examining him and by failing to properly prepare an SBI chemist as a defense expert where defendant suffered no prejudice).

[16] Failure to Move for or Obtain a Continuance[3]

State v. Frazier, 142 N.C. App. 361, 370, 542 S.E.2d 682, 689 (2001) (counsel was not ineffective by failing to move for a continuance and thus waiving defendant's statutory right not to be tried in the same week of arraignment; defendant provided no evidence that counsel's failure to move for a continuance impacted trial preparation

---

3. For cases addressing defendants' claims that they were denied their right to effective assistance because the trial court failed to grant motions to continue, see *infra* § 2.08[2].

and thus there was no reasonable possibility that had the motion been made, a different result would have been reached at trial).

In re **Clapp**, 137 N.C. App. 14, 25–26, 526 S.E.2d 689, 697–98 (2000) (rejecting juvenile's argument that dispositional attorney was ineffective by failing to move for a continuance on grounds that the court had not received sufficient social, medical, psychiatric, psychological, and educational information; counsel had already requested and received two continuances in order to secure the juvenile's presence, counsel filed a notice of appeal and a motion for appropriate relief after the dispositional hearing, and counsel presented evidence and argued vigorously at the hearing on the motion).

State v. Teasley, 82 N.C. App. 150, 159, 346 S.E.2d 227, 232 (1986) (counsel was not ineffective by failing to obtain a continuance made on grounds that he did not have an opportunity to prepare a defense; contrary to defendant's allegations, counsel had more than a day to prepare and defendant offered no evidence that counsel's performance suffered from the denial of a continuance).

[17]   Failure to Request Recording of Proceedings

State v. Hardison, 326 N.C. 646, 660–62, 392 S.E.2d 364, 372–73 (1990) (counsel was not ineffective by failing to request recordation of jury selection, bench conferences, and opening and closing arguments; in noncapital cases, transcripts are not required for jury selection or opening and closing arguments; defendant's argument that without a record of the bench conferences he could not effectively evaluate issues for appeal failed because he made no attempt to reconstruct the record of the conferences and made "no specific allegation" of error as to them).

State v. Swann, 322 N.C. 666, 685, 370 S.E.2d 533, 544 (1988) (counsel was not ineffective by failing to move to request the complete recordation of the trial, including jury selection; the court rejected defendant's contention that if the recording had been made he might have been able to establish a *Batson* claim because the case was tried before *Batson* was decided).

[18]   Court's Failure to Grant Request for *ex Parte* Hearing on Need for
       Expert Assistance

State v. Bates, 333 N.C. 523, 527, 428 S.E.2d 693, 695 (1993) (trial court's denial of capital defendant's pretrial motion for an *ex parte* hearing regarding his request for the assistance of a forensic psychologist jeopardized, among other rights, defendant's right to effective assistance; such an error cannot be found harmless; new trial).

State v. Ballard, 333 N.C. 515, 516–23, 428 S.E.2d 178, 179–83 (1993) (holding that by denying defendant's motion for an *ex parte* hearing of evidence supporting his request for the assistance of a psychiatric expert, the trial court jeopardized defendant's rights, including his right to effective assistance of counsel; "[b]ecause we cannot know what defendant would have presented in support of his request had he not been required to make his showing in open court, we cannot say that the error was harmless beyond a reasonable doubt"; new trial) (footnote omitted).

State v. Phipps, 331 N.C. 427, 447–51, 418 S.E.2d 178, 188–91 (1992) (rejecting indigent defendant's contention that the trial court violated his right to effective assistance by denying his motion for an *ex parte* hearing on his need for expert assistance on fingerprint identification; defendant had no constitutional right under *Ake v. Oklahoma*, 470 U.S. 68 (1985), or otherwise to the *ex parte* hearing).

[19] Withdrawal or Discharge of Counsel

State v. Nelson, 76 N.C. App. 371, 372–74, 333 S.E.2d 499, 500–02 (1985) (trial court violated defendant's right to effective assistance by *ex mero motu* discharging his appointed counsel on the eve of trial and requiring defendant, against his wishes, to be represented by counsel retained by his relatives; there was no justifiable cause for discharging defendant's counsel of choice and no finding that defendant's indigent status had changed), *modified and aff'd*, 316 N.C. 350, 341 S.E.2d 561 (1986).

State v. Cole, 343 N.C. 399, 411, 471 S.E.2d 362, 367 (1996) (defendant was not denied effective assistance when the trial court denied counsel's motion to withdraw made one week before trial; counsel zealously represented defendant, any disputes between counsel and defendant were resolved before trial, and there was no indication that defendant refused to cooperate with counsel).

State v. Robinson, 330 N.C. 1, 10–12, 409 S.E.2d 288, 293–94 (1991) (rejecting defendant's argument that the trial court violated his right to effective assistance by refusing to remove his court-appointed counsel for reasons of distrust stemming from their decision to send him for a forensic examination without his consent; defendant failed to show any impediment to his defense caused by the tactical decision to have the examination).

State v. Kuplen, 316 N.C. 387, 393–99, 343 S.E.2d 793, 796–800 (1986) (rejecting defendant's contention that he was denied effective assistance of counsel when the trial judge refused to allow defendant's court-appointed lawyer to withdraw and refused to appoint new counsel; no evidence was offered justifying replacement of appointed counsel).

State v. Cobb, 150 N.C. App. 31, 35–36, 563 S.E.2d 600, 604–05 (2002) (rejecting defendant's argument that his right to effective assistance was violated when the trial court denied his motion to remove one of his court-appointed lawyers; counsel was "clearly qualified" to represent defendant and any conflicts between defendant and counsel related to trial strategy and did not warrant removal), *review denied*, 356 N.C. 169 (2002).

[20] Miscellaneous Pretrial Claims

State v. Jones, 347 N.C. 193, 206–11, 491 S.E.2d 641, 649–52 (1997) (rejecting defendant's argument that the trial court's alleged improper and disrespectful conduct toward defendant's counsel by making insulting and sarcastic comments violated his right to effective assistance; the trial court's conduct was not improper, and even if it was, defendant failed to show prejudice).

State v. Bailey, 145 N.C. App. 13, 23, 548 S.E.2d 814, 820–21 (2001) (rejecting defendant's argument that counsel was ineffective by not limiting the extent of his representation pursuant to G.S. 15A-141 and "thereby rendering defendant vulnerable to the consequences of representation by inexperienced counsel"; defendant failed to establish any particular error committed by counsel that affected the outcome of the trial).

State v. Wilfong, 101 N.C. App. 221, 224, 398 S.E.2d 668, 670–71 (1990) (counsel was not ineffective by failing to make arrangements for a lineup after defendant requested that counsel do so; defendant did not show why he was entitled to a lineup or how not having one prejudiced his case).

§ 2.02 Alleged Ineffectiveness in Connection with Guilty Pleas and Plea Bargains

[1] Incorrect or Deficient Advice

State v. Taylor, 141 N.C. App. 321, 323–28, 541 S.E.2d 199, 200–03 (2000) (counsel was not ineffective by (1) failing to review the possible sentences with defendant so that she could make an educated and informed decision whether to accept a plea bargain or proceed with trial and (2) providing defendant with deficient information resulting in her failure to accept a plea bargain; even if counsel's conduct was deficient, defendant was not prejudiced because both alleged deficiencies were corrected on the record "by the trial judge's clear, deliberate steps to explain the sentence and plea to defendant"), *cert. denied*, 355 N.C. 499, 564 S.E.2d 231 (2002).

State v. Goforth, 130 N.C. App. 603, 603–06, 503 S.E.2d 676, 677–79 (1998) (counsel's erroneous advice that defendant could appeal her sentence to superior court was deficient but not prejudicial where defendant "fail[ed] utterly to allege or show that, but for the misadvice of counsel, she would not have entered a guilty plea, and would have proceeded to a trial on the merits").

State v. Wilkins, 131 N.C. App. 220, 225, 506 S.E.2d 274, 277 (1998) (defendant was not denied effective assistance of counsel in connection with her guilty plea; the following "ample evidence" supported the trial judge's findings and conclusion that counsel was not ineffective: (1) counsel met with defendant on several occasions and discussed a plea offer, which defendant rejected; (2) counsel conducted a mock trial at which the jurors decided against defendant; (3) thereafter defendant decided to plead guilty and counsel prepared a transcript of plea, went over each question with her, and wrote down her answers; (4) counsel advised defendant that she could receive the active sentence that was ultimately imposed; and (5) defendant indicated to the judge that she was satisfied with counsel's services when questioned by the trial judge).

State v. Dammons, 128 N.C. App. 16, 24, 493 S.E.2d 480, 485 (1997) (rejecting defendant's argument that had counsel performed adequate research and determined that a prior conviction violated *Boykin*, defendant would not have pleaded guilty to a later habitual felon conviction where the *Boykin* claim was without merit).

State v. Lesane, 137 N.C. App. 234, 244–45, 528 S.E.2d 37, 44 (2000) (counsel's incorrect understanding regarding the applicable punishment for first-degree murder in connection with plea discussions did not amount to ineffective assistance where defendant did not suggest that the error had any effect on plea discussions and his decision not to take a plea).

[2]   Failure to Communicate Plea Offer to the Defendant or Acceptance to the Prosecutor[4]

State v. Martin, 318 N.C. 648, 649–52, 350 S.E.2d 63, 64–65 (1986) (trial judge did not abuse his discretion in denying defendant's claim that counsel was ineffective by failing to communicate a plea offer made by the district attorney; defendant offered "no evidence that a definitive plea offer was ever made").

State v. Johnson, 126 N.C. App. 271, 485 S.E.2d 315 (1997) (rejecting defendant's claim that counsel was ineffective by failing to timely communicate defendant's acceptance of a plea agreement; even if counsel had timely communicated defendant's acceptance, the prosecutor would not have presented the proposed agreement to the court because after offering it, he discovered that the defendant had substantial criminal history).

[3]   *Harbison* Claims: Admission of Guilt in Connection with a Guilty Plea

State v. Morganherring, 350 N.C. 701, 711–20, 517 S.E.2d 622, 628–33 (1999) (counsel was not ineffective by advising capital defendant, who executed a *Harbison* statement consenting to a change in defense theories and who was examined on the issue by the court, to (1) withdraw plea of not guilty by reason of insanity to murder charge and (2) plead guilty to sexual offense charges and not guilty to murder charges that were based in part on the felony murder theory; defendant failed to show that he was prejudiced by any deficient performance of counsel in view of the fact that he had no realistic defense to the sexual offense charges and hence no defense to first-degree felony murder, he was subject to felony murder by way of an additional robbery charge, and he was also convicted of murder on the basis of premeditation and deliberation), *cert. denied,* 529 U.S. 1024 (2000).[5]

[4]   Miscellaneous Guilty Plea Claims

State v. Bailey, 145 N.C. App. 13, 23, 548 S.E.2d 814, 821 (2001) (rejecting defendant's argument that counsel was ineffective by failing to require the State to follow the mandate of G.S. 15A-1023 and modify the terms of a plea arrangement after the arrangement has been rejected; G.S. 15A-1023 does not require the State to make such a modification).

---

4. In *State v. Simmons,* 65 N.C. App. 294, 300, 309 S.E.2d 493, 497 (1983), a case decided before *State v. Braswell,* 312 N.C. 553, 324 S.E.2d 241 (1985), the court held that failure to inform a client of a plea offer constitutes IAC, absent extenuating circumstances.

5. *See supra* pp. 48–49 (discussing *Harbison* in detail).

§ 2.03 Ineffectiveness at Trial[6]

[1]   Failure to Pursue Defenses

[a]   Failure to Pursue Alibi Defense

State v. Swann, 322 N.C. 666, 682, 370 S.E.2d 533, 542 (1988) (counsel's failure to pursue an alibi defense by not interviewing defendant's mother was not unreasonable where defendant told counsel that he did not know where he was at the time of the crimes; the record supported the trial court's conclusion that the mother's testimony that defendant was with her at the time of the incidents was "inherently incredible" given the fact that she did not give the information to counsel or come to trial).

State v. Lowery, 318 N.C. 54, 69, 347 S.E.2d 729, 739 (1986) (counsel was not ineffective by failing to develop alibi witnesses; counsel attempted to develop the defense by calling two witnesses, both of whom were substantially discredited by the State; the reviewing court refused to "substitute [its] judgment for that of trial counsel as to whether other alibi witnesses, if available, would have been helpful").

State v. Dockery, 78 N.C. App. 190, 191–92, 336 S.E.2d 719, 721 (1985) (counsel was not ineffective by failing to pursue an alibi defense; because defendant presented no evidence concerning the validity of the defense, there was no basis to hold that defendant was prejudiced by counsel's alleged deficiency).

State v. Gary, 348 N.C. 510, 514–16, 501 S.E.2d 57, 61–62 (1998) (counsel was not ineffective by failing to issue process for or call an alibi witness; the disagreement between counsel and defendant over the tactical issue of whether the witnesses would be helpful did not require that counsel be replaced).

[b]   Failure to Pursue Self-Defense

State v. Lesane, 137 N.C. App. 234, 246–47, 528 S.E.2d 37, 45 (2000) (refusing to question counsel's strategic decision not to pursue imperfect self-defense where doing so would have required defendant to take the stand and contradict an "abundance of testimony"; alternatively, no prejudice resulted from counsel's decision to forgo this defense "in light of the overwhelming evidence of defendant's guilt").

[c]   Failure to Pursue Insanity Defense

State v. Attmore, 92 N.C. App. 385, 391–94, 374 S.E.2d 649, 653–55 (1988) (counsel was not ineffective by failing to pursue an insanity defense; counsel's conduct was not deficient where defendant offered nothing to put counsel on notice that he needed to explore whether the defense existed; even if counsel's performance was deficient, no prejudice resulted where the State's case against defendant was "strong").

[d]   Miscellaneous Failure to Pursue Defense Cases

State v. Piche, 102 N.C. App. 630, 638–39, 403 S.E.2d 559, 564 (1991) (rejecting

---

6. For cases dealing with claims of ineffectiveness in connection with withdrawal or discharge of counsel, see *supra* § 2.01[19].

defendant's claim that counsel was ineffective by failing to prepare a defense where defendant did not "refer[] to any defense which would have changed the outcome of defendant's trial").

[2]   Jury Selection[7]

State v. Rogers, 355 N.C. 420, 449–50, 562 S.E.2d 859, 878 (2002) (rejecting capital defendant's claim that counsel was ineffective by not objecting when the trial court excused two prospective jurors solely on account of their age; trial court's action was proper and in any event no prejudice resulted from counsel's failure to object where "the evidence of . . . guilt was strong" and there was no evidence "suggesting that the two jurors who were excused would have led the other jurors to a different verdict if they had been selected to sit on this case").

State v. Jaynes, 353 N.C. 534, 547–48, 549 S.E.2d 179, 191 (2001) (rejecting defendant's assertion that counsel was ineffective by failing to use a peremptory challenge against a juror; based on the facts, counsel's decision to refrain from using the challenge "could very well have been a valid tactical choice and thus counsel's conduct cannot be found to be deficient"), *cert. denied*, 122 S. Ct. 1310 (2002).

State v. Blakeney, 352 N.C. 287, 307–09, 531 S.E.2d 799, 814–15 (2000) (holding that because defendant did not demonstrate and the record did not reveal that a prima facie case of racial discrimination in jury selection could have been made, counsel's failure to raise a *Batson* objection does not constitute ineffectiveness), *cert. denied*, 531 U.S. 1117 (2001).

State v. Frye, 341 N.C. 470, 492–93, 461 S.E.2d 664, 674–75 (1995) (rejecting capital defendant's claim that the trial court violated his right to effective assistance by allowing only one of his attorneys to conduct *voir dire*; concluding that even if the issue had been preserved for review, it would fail because "an indigent defendant's right to the appointment of *additional* counsel in capital cases is statutory, not constitutional") (quotation omitted).

State v. Ali, 329 N.C. 394, 402–04, 407 S.E.2d 183, 188–90 (1991) (rejecting defendant's argument that he was denied the right to effective assistance when the trial court and his attorneys allowed him to make the decision not to peremptorily challenge a juror his attorneys had wanted him to remove; counsel properly followed defendant's wishes after a record of absolute impasse was made).

State v. Shaw, 322 N.C. 797, 807–08, 370 S.E.2d 546, 552 (1988) (trial court's refusal to allow defendant's brother to sit at counsel's table and assist counsel during jury selection did not deprive defendant of effective assistance; defendant suffered no prejudice where the seating arrangement did not actually or constructively prevent his brother from communicating with defense counsel).

State v. Roper, 328 N.C. 337, 354–55, 402 S.E.2d 600, 610 (1991) (rejecting defendant's contention that he was denied his right to effective assistance when the trial

---

7. For a case dealing with an alleged concession of guilt during jury selection, see *State v. Strickland*, 346 N.C. 443, 488 S.E.2d 194 (1997), discussed *infra* p. 81.

court supplemented the jury venire with venire persons who had been sitting in a different courtroom).

[3]   Opening Statements[8]

State v. Moorman, 320 N.C. 387, 392–402, 358 S.E.2d 502, 506–13 (1987) (counsel's failure to produce evidence promised in his opening statement, coupled with counsel's closing argument that an important part of defendant's testimony was not credible, his regular use of a variety of painkilling drugs, his frequent migraines, and his drowsiness, lethargy, and inattentiveness during trial constituted ineffectiveness).

State v. Baker, 109 N.C. App. 643, 645–50, 428 S.E.2d 476, 477–80 (1993) (counsel was ineffective by incorrectly stating during his opening statement and while examining a witness that defendant had no prior criminal record; counsel's misstatements "led directly" to introduction of evidence that would not have been otherwise admissible; also, counsel did not object to a jury instruction providing that the jurors could consider the defendant's prior convictions to impeach his credibility even though they were admitted for the limited purpose of dispelling the false impression counsel inadvertently created with his remarks).

State v. Wiley, 355 N.C. 592, 618–20, 565 S.E.2d 22, 41–42 (2002) (rejecting defendant's argument that counsel made an unconsented-to admission in her opening; counsel did not concede that defendant was at the crime scene, and although counsel arguably signaled that some physical evidence linked defendant to the killing, she made clear it was of dubious validity; in context, her statements were not an admission), *petition for cert. filed* (Oct. 16, 2002) (No. 02-7017).

State v. Mason, 337 N.C. 165, 176–78, 446 S.E.2d 58, 64–65 (1994) (counsel was not ineffective by failing to present evidence to support a defense forecast in her opening statement; although counsel was not able to convince the jury to accept the defense, there was evidence supporting it and the counsel's opening remarks were not a "promised defense" as in *State v. Moorman*, 320 N.C. 387, 358 S.E.2d 502 (1987) (discussed above)).

State v. Swann, 322 N.C. 666, 687, 370 S.E.2d 533, 545 (1988) (counsel's failure to make an opening statement was not per se unreasonable; counsel made a tactical decision to forego an opening because he was uncertain what evidence would be introduced at trial and whether the victim would testify; court declined to review this tactical choice).

State v. Strickland, 346 N.C. 443, 454–55, 488 S.E.2d 194, 200–01 (1997) (counsel was not ineffective by making numerous assertions in his opening statement for which there was no supporting evidence and by admitting that defendant had a criminal record; the challenged assertions were part of a "reasonable tactic" to explain defendant's conduct and counsel "could have thought" that they would have been supported by eyewitness testimony; counsel could reasonably have decided to reveal

---

8. For a case dealing with an alleged concession of guilt during opening statements, see *State v. Basden*, 339 N.C. 288, 451 S.E.2d 238 (1994), discussed *infra* p. 82.

defendant's prior history in his opening to "lessen the impact" when it came in at trial; even if counsel's performance was deficient, no prejudice resulted because the evidence against the defendant was "overwhelming").

State v. Lewis, 321 N.C. 42, 46–49, 361 S.E.2d 728, 730–32 (1987) (counsel was not ineffective by making misstatements during his opening that permitted the prosecutor to disclose to the jury that defendant had previously been arrested, a fact the jury allegedly would not have otherwise known; given the context, the error was not "so serious" that counsel was not functioning as counsel guaranteed by the Sixth Amendment).

[4] Failure to Object to the Introduction of Evidence and Failure to Move to Strike Evidence

State v. Gainey, 355 N.C. 73, 112–13, 558 S.E.2d 463, 488 (2002) (rejecting defendant's argument that counsel was ineffective by failing to object to the admission of defendant's statements, jury instructions, and verdict sheets; counsel's failure to object did not constitute deficient conduct; because evidence of guilt was "overwhelming," counsel's failure to object did not cause prejudice), *cert. denied,* 123 S. Ct. 182 (2002).

State v. Lee, 348 N.C. 474, 491–93, 501 S.E.2d 334, 345–46 (1998) (counsel was not ineffective by failing to object to character and hearsay evidence; all but one item of the character evidence was admissible; as to the one inadmissible item of character evidence, defendant could not show that its admission deprived him of a fair trial; all but one item of the hearsay evidence was admissible; as to the one inadmissible item of hearsay evidence, its admission was harmless error and did not deprive defendant of a fair trial).

State v. Mason, 337 N.C. 165, 170–76, 446 S.E.2d 58, 64 (1994) (counsel was not ineffective by failing to object to evidence when all of the evidence was either admissible and/or no prejudice resulted from its admission).

State v. Lowery, 318 N.C. 54, 67–68, 347 S.E.2d 729, 738–39 (1986) (counsel was not ineffective by failing to object to hearsay testimony where statements were admissible).

State v. Braswell, 312 N.C. 553, 564–65, 324 S.E.2d 241, 249 (1985) (rejecting defendant's claim that counsel was ineffective by not vigorously opposing the introduction of statements defendant made to officers, not vigorously objecting to the introduction into evidence of three letters written by defendant implying that he intended to kill his wife, and allowing the introduction of other letters and a cassette recording that was not dated to show motive and state of mind; defendant suffered no prejudice).

State v. Stroud, 147 N.C. App. 549, 555–56, 557 S.E.2d 544, 548 (2001) (holding that defendant prematurely asserted on direct appeal a claim that trial counsel was ineffective by failing to object to evidence and request limiting instructions; dismissing the claim without prejudice to defendant's right to assert it in a motion for appropriate relief).

State v. Jones, 146 N.C. App. 394, 400, 553 S.E.2d 79, 83 (2001) (rejecting defendant's claim that counsel was ineffective by failing to object to testimony regarding the fact that defendant had invoked his right to remain silent and to have counsel present during questioning; although admission of the testimony was error, defendant could not show prejudice), *cert. denied*, 355 N.C. 754, 566 S.E.2d 83 (2002).

State v. Linton, 145 N.C. App. 639, 647–49, 551 S.E.2d 572, 577–78 (2001) (rejecting defendant's argument that counsel was ineffective by failing to object to hearsay testimony; no prejudice resulted because the testimony was "extremely similar" to other admissible statements and other evidence of defendant's guilt was "more than substantial"), *review denied*, 355 N.C. 498, 564 S.E.2d 229 (2002).

State v. Smith, 139 N.C. App. 209, 215, 533 S.E.2d 518, 521 (counsel was not ineffective, in part, by failing to object to an allegedly improper question posed by the prosecution during direct examination of the victim when the evidence that was obtained as a result of the question came in earlier in the trial), *appeal dismissed*, 353 N.C. 277, 546 S.E.2d 391 (2000).

State v. Jones, 137 N.C. App. 221, 232–34, 527 S.E.2d 700, 707–08 (2000) (counsel was not ineffective by failing to object to the State's evidence; some of the evidence was admissible; admission of other evidence was error but defendant corrected that error by offering similar testimony during his own cross-examination; regarding evidence that was inadmissible and not corrected, no prejudice resulted because the jury could have based its verdict on other admissible evidence, other evidence reduced any prejudice suffered, and the jury could not have found defendant guilty solely on the basis of the erroneously admitted evidence), *review denied*, 352 N.C. 153, 544 S.E.2d 235 (2000), *habeas corpus denied*, 544 S.E.2d 566 (2000).

State v. McGraw, 137 N.C. App. 726, 731–32, 529 S.E.2d 493, 498 (2000) (counsel was not ineffective by failing to object to police officer's testimony that was admitted to corroborate the child victim's testimony but was different from the child's testimony; although the officer's testimony did not precisely reflect the victim's testimony, it confirmed and strengthened her testimony and therefore was properly admitted for corroborative purposes), *review denied*, 352 N.C. 360, 544 S.E.2d 544 (2000).

State v. Broome, 136 N.C. App. 82, 92, 523 S.E.2d 448, 455–56 (1999) (rejecting defendant's arguments that counsel was ineffective by failing to object to witness's testimony on grounds it was not within witness's personal knowledge where testimony was based on personal knowledge), *review denied*, 351 N.C. 362, 543 S.E.2d 136 (2000).

State v. Pretty, 134 N.C. App. 379, 387–89, 517 S.E.2d 677, 683–84 (counsel was not ineffective by failing to object to a social worker's testimony that the child victim's statements were believable because defense counsel opened the door to the testimony and it was thus admissible; apparently defendant did not argue that counsel was ineffective by opening the door to the testimony), *review denied*, 351 N.C. 117, 540 S.E.2d 745 (1991), *writ denied*, 542 S.E.2d 664 (2000) *and* 570 S.E.2d 112 (2002).

State v. Davis, 130 N.C. App. 675, 680, 505 S.E.2d 138, 142 (1998) (rejecting defendant's contention that counsel was ineffective by failing to object to publication of a witness's handwritten statement and to move to strike testimony where statement and testimony were admissible).

State v. Poe, 119 N.C. App. 266, 272–73, 458 S.E.2d 242, 246–47 (1995) (rejecting defendant's argument that counsel was ineffective by failing to object to prior bad act testimony where testimony was properly admitted).

State v. Howie, 116 N.C. App. 609, 614–15, 448 S.E.2d 867, 870 (1994) (declining to address the details of defendant's argument that counsel "facilitated the admission of prejudicial and oftentimes incompetent evidence" where there was "overwhelming evidence" of guilt and "no possibility" that the jury would have reached a different verdict but for counsel's alleged errors).

State v. Baker, 109 N.C. App. 643, 645, 428 S.E.2d 476, 477–78 (1993) (counsel was not ineffective by failing to object to evidence of penetration where the evidence was relevant to the charge of indecent liberties with a child).[9]

State v. Summers, 92 N.C. App. 453, 458–59, 374 S.E.2d 631, 635 (1988) (counsel was not ineffective by failing to have Rule 404(b) evidence excluded from trial where evidence was admissible).

State v. Durham, 74 N.C. App. 201, 204–05, 328 S.E.2d 304, 306–07 (1985) (rejecting defendant's claim that counsel was ineffective by objecting only once at trial, failing to produce witnesses, and failing to move for dismissal; defendant failed to show that counsel's errors, if any, deprived him of a fair trial).

State v. Aiken, 73 N.C. App. 487, 493–95, 326 S.E.2d 919, 923–24 (1985) (counsel was not ineffective by failing to object to hearsay evidence that was impermissible, but not prejudicial; counsel was not ineffective at rape trial by failing to object to testimony regarding defendant's race where no prejudice resulted).

[5]   Witnesses

[a]   Failure to Move to Disqualify Witnesses

In re **Clapp**, 137 N.C. App. 14, 25, 526 S.E.2d 689, 697 (2000) (adjudicatory attorney was not ineffective by failing to move to disqualify child witnesses on grounds they were incompetent to testify; attorney could have determined that a court would find the witnesses competent to testify and that an objection as to competency, if overruled, could only enhance their credibility; even if counsel's performance was deficient, no prejudice resulted "given the likelihood" that the hearsay statements made by the children would have been admitted as substantive evidence).

[b]   Failure to Object to the State's Examination of Witnesses

State v. Braswell, 312 N.C. 553, 565–66, 324 S.E.2d 241, 250 (1985) (rejecting defendant's argument that counsel was ineffective by failing to timely object to the State's cross-examination of a defense expert regarding experiments conducted with the murder weapon where defendant suffered no prejudice).

[c]   Failure to Call or Recall Witnesses

State v. Gary, 348 N.C. 510, 514–16, 501 S.E.2d 57, 61–62 (1998) (counsel was not ineffective by failing to issue process for or call an alibi witness so as to require appointment of substitute counsel; which witnesses to call is a matter of trial tactics).

---

9. In *Baker*, counsel was found to be ineffective on other grounds. *See infra* p. 75.

State v. Campbell, 142 N.C. App. 145, 151–53, 541 S.E.2d 803, 807 (2001) (counsel was not ineffective by failing to recall witnesses where counsel made a "reasoned strategy decision" based on the belief that recalling the witnesses would "underline things and just make things worse" (counsel decided that posing further questions to a child victim who had already cried on the stand "would not yield a gain equal to the damage done if the jury were made more sympathetic to the alleged victim"); nothing in the record indicated that re-examining the witnesses would have resulted in a different outcome).

State v. Broome, 136 N.C. App. 82, 91–92, 523 S.E.2d 448, 455–56 (1999) (rejecting defendant's contention that counsel was ineffective by failing to locate, recall, and cross-examine the State's key witness upon discovering the terms of a witness-informant's plea agreement; the court was not persuaded that the outcome of the trial was affected by defense counsel's alleged failings), *review denied*, 351 N.C. 362, 543 S.E.2d 136 (2000).

State v. Durham, 74 N.C. App. 201, 204–05, 328 S.E.2d 304, 307 (1985) (rejecting defendant's claim that counsel was ineffective by, among other things, failing to produce witnesses where defendant did not show that this error deprived him of a fair trial).

[d]   Examination and Cross-Examination of Witnesses or the Defendant

State v. Baker, 109 N.C. App. 643, 645–50, 428 S.E.2d 476, 477–80 (1993) (counsel was ineffective by incorrectly stating during his opening statement and while examining a witness that defendant had no prior criminal record; counsel's misstatements "led directly" to introduction of evidence that would not have been otherwise admissible; also, counsel did not object to a jury instruction providing that the jurors could consider the defendant's prior convictions to impeach his credibility even though they were admitted for the limited purpose of dispelling the false impression counsel inadvertently created with his remarks).

State v. Call, 353 N.C. 400, 413–15, 545 S.E.2d 190, 199–200 (2001) (rejecting capital defendant's claim that the trial court violated his right to effective assistance by permitting only one of his attorneys to object during the prosecutor's direct examination of a witness; holding that even if defendant had properly preserved the issue for appeal, it would fail because an indigent defendant's right to the appointment of *additional* counsel in capital cases is statutory, not constitutional), *cert. denied*, 122 S. Ct. 628 (2001).

State v. Lowery, 318 N.C. 54, 68, 347 S.E.2d 729, 739 (1986) (holding that counsel was not ineffective in his examination of witnesses and declining to "second-guess" counsel's trial strategy).

State v. McMillian, 147 N.C. App. 707, 714–15, 557 S.E.2d 138, 144 (2001) (rejecting defendant's argument that counsel was ineffective by eliciting evidence regarding defendant's use of a dangerous weapon, an element of the offense that the State allegedly had failed to show; the State presented sufficient evidence on direct examination of the use of a dangerous weapon and thus defendant failed to show deficient performance or prejudice stemming from counsel's cross-examination), *review denied*, 355 N.C. 219, 560 S.E.2d 152 (2002).

State v. Montford, 137 N.C. App. 495, 503, 529 S.E.2d 247, 253 (counsel was not ineffective by failing to cross-examine a detective about an issue; given the wide latitude afforded to counsel in matters regarding cross-examination, counsel's failure to cross-examine the witness on this issue did not render his assistance constitutionally defective), *cert. denied*, 353 N.C. 275, 546 S.E.2d 386 (2000).

State v. Smith, 139 N.C. App. 209, 215, 533 S.E.2d 518, 521 (counsel was not ineffective, in part, by cross-examining the victim in such a way as to elicit incriminating evidence where the evidence obtained as a result of the cross-examination had been presented earlier in the trial in response to a question posed by the prosecutor), *appeal dismissed*, 353 N.C. 277, 546 S.E.2d 391 (2000).

State v. Broome, 136 N.C. App. 82, 91–92, 523 S.E.2d 448, 455–56 (1999) (rejecting defendant's contention that counsel was ineffective by failing to locate, recall, and cross-examine the State's key witness upon discovering the terms of a witness-informant's plea agreement; the court was not persuaded that the outcome of the trial was affected by defense counsel's alleged failings), *review denied*, 351 N.C. 362, 543 S.E.2d 136 (2000).

State v. Swindler, 129 N.C. App. 1, 10, 497 S.E.2d 318, 323–24 (1998) (rejecting defendant's argument that the trial judge erred in denying his motion for a mistrial; mistrial motion asserted that counsel was ineffective by failing to cross-examine several witnesses about matters that allegedly would have exposed inconsistencies in the State's case; the court stated simply: "We have examined the record and hold that defendant has made no showing whatever that his counsel's performance was objectively unreasonable."), *aff'd*, 349 N.C. 347, 507 S.E.2d 284 (1998).

State v. Jones, 97 N.C. App. 189, 202–03, 388 S.E.2d 213, 220–21 (1990) (rejecting defendant's argument that counsel was ineffective by failing to cross-examine witness in "a sufficient manner" where defendant did not indicate what matters counsel failed to inquire into on cross-examination).

State v. Seagroves, 78 N.C. App. 49, 54, 336 S.E.2d 684, 668 (1985) (counsel was not ineffective by failing to adequately cross-examine a guard regarding his prior inconsistent statement; the record showed that counsel established the fact of the prior inconsistent statement through his cross-examination; even if counsel should have cross-examined the guard further, failure to do so did not amount to a failure to function as counsel).

State v. Aiken, 73 N.C. App. 487, 495–96, 326 S.E.2d 919, 924 (1985) (counsel was not ineffective by conducting only a brief direct and redirect examination of defendant; counsel's examinations of defendant adequately presented the defense theory).

State v. Braswell, 312 N.C. 553, 565, 324 S.E.2d 241, 249–50 (1985) (rejecting defendant's claim that counsel was ineffective by failing to adequately cross-examine defendant's son and by eliciting during cross-examination adverse testimony; no prejudice resulted, because evidence was cumulative).

[6]   **Failure to Present Evidence or to Present Evidence Sufficiently**

State v. Lancaster, 137 N.C. App. 37, 49–50, 537 S.E.2d 61, 69–70 (2000) (rejecting defendant's claim that counsel was ineffective by failing to submit into evidence an SBI lab report of defendant's DNA and additional medical records regarding defendant's drug use and addiction; counsel's decisions were "strategic" and neither "approach the levels required by *Braswell*"), *review allowed in part, denied in part*, 352 N.C. 680, 545 S.E.2d 723 (2000).

State v. Jones, 97 N.C. App. 189, 202–03, 388 S.E.2d 213, 220–21 (1990) (rejecting defendant's argument that counsel was ineffective by failing to present evidence where defendant did not indicate what evidence counsel failed to present and where counsel "vigorously opposed the admission of [damaging] evidence . . . and he could do little else in view of the strength of that evidence").

State v. Oxendine, 112 N.C. App. 731, 734–37, 436 S.E.2d 906, 909–11 (1993) (counsel was not ineffective by failing to present evidence; the State's case was entirely circumstantial and counsel apparently made a reasonable strategic judgment that the jury would not convict based solely on circumstantial evidence; defendant's own exculpatory statements were put to the jury, the usefulness of her potential defense witnesses was "questionable at best," and by deciding not to present evidence, counsel gained the tactical advantage of being allowed to open and close oral arguments to the jury).

[7] Allowing Proceedings to Occur in the Defendant's Absence

State v. Braswell, 312 N.C. 553, 564, 324 S.E.2d 241, 249 (1985) (rejecting defendant's argument that counsel was ineffective by allowing a *voir dire* hearing on a witness's testimony to be held in defendant's absence where defendant suffered no prejudice).

[8] Failure to Move for Mistrial

State v. Davis, 130 N.C. App. 675, 680, 505 S.E.2d 138, 142 (1998) (rejecting defendant's contention that counsel was ineffective by failing to move for a mistrial after portions of a witness's testimony were withdrawn where curative instruction addressed any error created by admission of the testimony).

State v. Poe, 119 N.C. App. 266, 272–73, 458 S.E.2d 242, 246–47 (1995) (rejecting defendant's argument that counsel was ineffective by failing to object and move for a mistrial after a witness was allowed to testify regarding a prior bad act allegedly committed by defendant where the prior bad act testimony was admissible).

[9] Failure to Move for Dismissal

In re **Clapp**, 137 N.C. App. 14, 23–25, 526 S.E.2d 689, 696–97 (2000) (juvenile's attorney was not ineffective by failing to move for a dismissal at the close of the State's evidence on grounds that there was insufficient evidence of force in connection with sex offense; even if counsel's performance was deficient, the juvenile was not prejudiced by it because sufficient evidence to withstand a motion to dismiss was presented during the hearing).

State v. Broome, 136 N.C. App. 82, 92, 523 S.E.2d 448, 455–56 (1999) (rejecting defendant's contention that counsel was ineffective by failing to renew his motion to dismiss on grounds of fatal variance between State's evidence and offense charged and insufficiency of the evidence where variance was not fatal and evidence was sufficient), *review denied*, 351 N.C. 362, 543 S.E.2d 136 (2000).

State v. Hinnant, 131 N.C. App. 591, 596–97, 508 S.E.2d 537, 540–41 (1998) (rejecting defendant's claim that counsel was ineffective by failing to move to dismiss at the close of all the evidence on grounds there was insufficient evidence of penetration to prove rape; defendant could not show that if the motion had been made, it would have been granted, in light of trial evidence on penetration issue), *aff'd in part, reversed in part on other grounds*, 351 N.C. 277, 523 S.E.2d 663 (2000).

State v. Davis, 130 N.C. App. 675, 680, 505 S.E.2d 138, 142 (1998) (rejecting defendant's claim that counsel was ineffective by failing to move for a mistrial when portions of a witness's testimony were withdrawn; the judge's curative instruction eliminated any prejudice caused by the testimony).

State v. Durham, 74 N.C. App. 201, 204–05 328 S.E.2d 304, 307 (1985) (rejecting defendant's claim that counsel was ineffective by failing to move for dismissal, objecting only once at trial, and failing to move for a mistrial where he made no showing that counsel's errors, if any, deprived him of a fair trial).

[10]   Ineffectiveness in Connection with Closing Arguments[10]

State v. Moorman, 320 N.C. 387, 392–402, 358 S.E.2d 502, 506–13 (1987) (counsel's failure to produce evidence promised in his opening statement, coupled with counsel's closing argument that an important part of defendant's testimony was not credible, his regular use of a variety of painkilling drugs, his frequent migraines, and his drowsiness, lethargy, and inattentiveness during trial constituted IAC).

State v. Bowman, 349 N.C. 459, 474–75, 509 S.E.2d 428, 438 (1998) (rejecting defendant's contention that he was deprived of effective assistance when the trial court sustained the prosecutor's objection to a portion of defense counsel's closing argument in which defense counsel argued his conception of reasonable doubt; the trial court properly sustained the prosecutor's objection to counsel's argument; even if the trial court erred in sustaining the objection, the error was cured when the court thereafter correctly instructed the jury on reasonable doubt).

State v. Gaines, 345 N.C. 647, 674–75, 483 S.E.2d 396, 412–13 (1997) (rejecting defendant's argument that his right to effective assistance was violated when the trial court failed to intervene *ex mero motu* after the prosecutor allegedly attacked defense counsel's integrity and credibility during the State's closing argument; since defendant did not object to the statements at trial, the standard is gross impropriety requiring intervention *ex mero motu*; comments were not grossly improper).

State v. Robinson, 339 N.C. 263, 280–82, 451 S.E.2d 196, 207–08 (1994) (rejecting capital defendant's argument that by sustaining the prosecutor's objections to certain portions of defense counsel's jury argument at sentencing phase, his right to effective assistance of counsel was violated; trial judge properly sustained prosecutor's objection to argument that was unsupported by evidence and to argument asking that jurors disregard the facts, speak from their hearts, and find "some reason on earth" to reject the death penalty).

---

10. For cases claiming IAC due to counsel's alleged admission of defendant's guilt in closing arguments, *see infra* § 2.03[13].

State v. Washington, 141 N.C. App. 354, 374, 540 S.E.2d 388, 401–02 (2000) (counsel was not ineffective by failing to object to portions of the State's closing argument referring to defendant's failure to claim self-defense before trial; in light of the "substantial" evidence of the defendant's guilt, there was no reasonable probability that counsel's failure to object affected the outcome of the trial), *review denied*, 353 N.C. 396, 547 S.E.2d 427 (2001).

[11]   Ineffectiveness in Connection with Charging the Jury or Dealing with the Jury[11]

State v. Baker, 109 N.C. App. 643, 645–50, 428 S.E.2d 476, 477–80 (1993) (counsel was ineffective by incorrectly stating during his opening statement and at other times in the trial that defendant had no prior criminal record; counsel's misstatements "led directly" to introduction of evidence that would not have been otherwise admissible; also, counsel did not object to a jury instruction providing that the jurors could consider the defendant's prior convictions to impeach his credibility even though they were admitted for the limited purpose of dispelling the false impression counsel inadvertently created with his remarks).

State v. Jones, 137 N.C. App. 221, 232–34, 527 S.E.2d 700, 707–08 (counsel was not ineffective by failing to object to a jury instruction where jury instruction was proper), *review denied*, 352 N.C. 153, 544 S.E.2d 235, *habeas corpus denied*, 544 S.E.2d 566 (2000).

State v. Broome, 136 N.C. App. 82, 92, 523 S.E.2d 448, 455–56 (1999) (rejecting defendant's contention that counsel was ineffective by failing to object to court's refusal to instruct on attempt and request an entrapment instruction where the trial judge properly refused to instruct on attempt and defendant was not entitled to entrapment instruction), *review denied*, 351 N.C. 362, 543 S.E.2d 136 (2000).

State v. Manley, 345 N.C. 484, 487, 480 S.E.2d 659, 661 (1997) (counsel was not ineffective by failing to object to the jury instructions and verdict sheet for first-degree murder on grounds that they allowed the jury to find defendant guilty without a unanimous verdict; there was no error in the instructions or the verdict sheet).

State v. Howie, 116 N.C. App. 609, 614–15, 448 S.E.2d 867, 870 (1994) (declining to consider the details of defendant's claim that counsel was ineffective by failing to request an instruction on a lesser-included offense where there was "overwhelming evidence" of guilt and "no possibility" that the jury would have reached a different verdict but for counsel's alleged errors).

State v. Aiken, 73 N.C. App. 487, 496, 499, 326 S.E.2d 919, 924, 926 (1985) (counsel was not ineffective by failing to object to a jury instruction in a rape case regarding the victim's intoxication where the instruction was proper).

State v. Swann, 322 N.C. 666, 687–88, 370 S.E.2d 533, 545–46 (1988) (counsel was not ineffective by failing to request six jury instructions; one instruction was improper; absence of the others in the jury charge did not result in plain error).

---

11. For cases claiming IAC due to counsel's alleged errors in connection with jury instructions specific to capital cases, *see infra* § 2.09.

State v. Montford, 137 N.C. App. 495, 502, 529 S.E.2d 247, 252 (counsel was not ineffective by failing to request that the jury be instructed on defendant's decision not to testify at trial; there was no plain error and counsel may have decided against the instruction so as not to emphasize defendant's silence), *cert. denied*, 353 N.C. 275, 546 S.E.2d 386 (2000).

State v. Smith, 139 N.C. App. 209, 215–16, 533 S.E.2d 518, 521 (counsel was not ineffective by failing to submit a written request for a jury instruction on misdemeanor disorderly conduct where it was unlikely that the request would have been granted because misdemeanor disorderly conduct was not a lesser-included offense of any charge for which defendant was tried), *appeal dismissed*, 353 N.C. 277, 546 S.E.2d 391 (2000).

State v. Seagroves, 78 N.C. App. 49, 54, 336 S.E.2d 684, 688 (1985) (counsel was not ineffective by failing to request certain jury instructions where there was no plain error in the instructions).

State v. Cogdell, 74 N.C. App. 647, 652, 329 S.E.2d 675, 678 (1985) (rejecting defendant's argument that counsel was ineffective by failing to object to a jury instruction that "he who hunts with the pack is responsible for the kill" where instruction was not error).

State v. Braswell, 312 N.C. 553, 564, 324 S.E.2d 241, 249 (1985) (rejecting defendant's claim that counsel was ineffective by failing to seek limiting instructions on letters written by defendant that implied that he intended to kill his wife; contrary to defendant's contentions, a proper foundation for admission of the letters was laid and they were relevant).

[12]   Counsel's Conduct in the Courtroom

State v. Blackwell, 133 N.C. App. 31, 37–38, 514 S.E.2d 116, 120–21 (1999) (defendant was not denied effective assistance when one of his attorneys walked out of court for no reason; counsel's actual performance did not fall below an objective standard of reasonableness).

State v. Edwards, 73 N.C. App. 599, 602–03, 327 S.E.2d 16, 18–19 (1985) (counsel was not ineffective because of his outburst in the courtroom (while the State was cross-examining defendant's alibi witness, counsel "raised up a group of papers and slammed them to the table . . . then stood up and addressed the court, interrupting the [prosecutor]"); although counsel's conduct "was unusual and unprofessional," nothing in the record suggested that "the isolated incident" affected the result of the trial).

[13]   *Harbison* Claims: Admission of Guilt at Trial[12]

State v. Harbison, 315 N.C. 175, 177–81, 337 S.E.2d 504, 505–08 (1985) (by admitting, without defendant's consent, defendant's guilt during closing arguments to the jury, counsel was ineffective per se and no specific prejudice need be established).

---

12. For cases dealing with allegations that counsel made unconsented-to admissions of guilt in capital sentencing proceedings, *see infra* § 2.09. For a case in which the defendant alleged that counsel made an unconsented-to admission of guilt in connection with a guilty plea, *see supra* § 2.02[3]

State v. Anderson, 355 N.C. 136, 143–44, 558 S.E.2d 87, 93 (2002) (counsel was not ineffective by admitting that defendant was responsible for cutting and strangling the victim where counsel repeatedly advised prospective jurors that these admissions did not admit first-degree murder; counsel did not explain that the admissions were not intended to concede guilt of rape or first-degree murder under murder by torture or felony murder theories).

State v. Gainey, 355 N.C. 73, 92–93, 558 S.E.2d 463, 476 (2002) (no admission of guilt of murder where counsel stated: "[I]f he's guilty of anything, he's guilty of accessory after the fact. He's guilty of possession of a stolen vehicle"; counsel's statement was not an admission that defendant was guilty of murder; defendant took the statement out of context; the consistent theory of the defense was that defendant was not guilty), *cert. denied*, 123 S. Ct. 182 (2002).

State v. Morganherring, 350 N.C. 701, 711–20, 517 S.E.2d 622, 628–33 (1999) (counsel was not ineffective by advising capital defendant, who executed a *Harbison* statement consenting to a change in defense theories, to (1) withdraw notice of and plea of not guilty by reason of insanity and instead plead not guilty to murder charges that were based, in part, on felony murder theory and (2) plead guilty to sexual offense charges; defendant was fully aware of the direct consequences of his plea, including that in all likelihood he would be convicted of first-degree murder under the felony murder theory; additionally, defendant failed to show that he was prejudiced by any deficient performance of counsel in view of the fact that he had "no realistic defense" to first-degree felony murder, that he was subject to felony murder by way of an additional robbery charge, and that he was also convicted of murder on the basis of premeditation and deliberation), *cert. denied*, 529 U.S. 1024 (2000).

State v. McNeill, 346 N.C. 233, 237–38, 485 S.E.2d 284, 286–87 (1997) (counsel was not ineffective in this capital case by admitting during closing argument that defendant was guilty of second-degree murder; counsel's argument was consistent with defendant's stipulation that he stabbed the victim and proximately caused her death; the trial court questioned defendant and found that defendant knowingly, voluntarily, and understandingly consented to the stipulation).

State v. Strickland, 346 N.C. 443, 453–54, 488 S.E.2d 194, 200 (1997) (counsel was not ineffective by stating during jury selection that capital defendant was holding the gun that killed the victim at the time the victim was shot; counsel's statements did not amount to an admission of defendant's guilt, but rather statements of uncontroverted evidence).

State v. Bishop, 343 N.C. 518, 542–43, 472 S.E.2d 842, 854 (1996) (rejecting capital defendant's claim that counsel conceded defendant's guilt of financial transaction card fraud without defendant's consent during his closing argument to the jury where counsel did not concede defendant's guilt as alleged).

State v. Hinson, 341 N.C. 66, 77–78, 459 S.E.2d 261, 268–69 (1995) (counsel was not ineffective by arguing in his closing that another man who was with defendant when the crime occurred was the guilty one; the record revealed that counsel never conceded that defendant himself committed any crime whatsoever).

State v. Basden, 339 N.C. 288, 299, 451 S.E.2d 238, 244 (1994) (rejecting capital defendant's claim that counsel was ineffective by admitting in his opening statement that defendant was guilty of second-degree murder or voluntary manslaughter; just before closing arguments defendant consented on the record to his attorney's concession of guilt and this consent ratified counsel's earlier concession and cured any possible error).

State v. Harvell, 334 N.C. 356, 361, 432 S.E.2d 125, 128 (1993) (rejecting defendant's argument that counsel was ineffective during closing by admitting guilt without defendant's consent; counsel did not concede guilt; counsel "merely noted that if the evidence tended to establish the commission of any crime, that crime was voluntary manslaughter").

State v. Greene, 332 N.C. 565, 570–72, 422 S.E.2d 730, 733–34 (1992) (rejecting defendant's claim that counsel was ineffective by arguing to the jury in his closing statement and without defendant's consent that the jury should find defendant guilty of involuntary manslaughter; in the first of two challenged statements, counsel did not ask the jury to find defendant guilty of involuntary manslaughter—rather, counsel stated that if he was guilty of anything, it was involuntary manslaughter; nothing in the second statement even "approache[d] an admission of guilt").

State v. McDowell, 329 N.C. 363, 385–88, 407 S.E.2d 200, 212–14 (1991) (counsel was not ineffective in his closing argument in guilt phase of a capital trial by conceding defendant's guilt to the jury because defendant consented to the admissions; before closings, the trial judge informed defendant of his need to authorize counsel to make any admission, gave him instructions on an unobtrusive way to stop any argument that went beyond the scope of his consent, and determined after the closing that counsel had said what defendant wished him to say; also concluding that counsel's admissions were arguably "a strategically reasonable argument").

State v. Thomas, 329 N.C. 423, 438–42, 407 S.E.2d 141, 151–54 (1991) (rejecting capital defendant's contention that counsel was ineffective by conceding during jury argument that defendant committed second-degree murder and completed at least one element of the sexual offense; defendant orally and in writing consented to the admission of guilt of second-degree murder and counsel did not concede defendant's guilt on the sexual offense charge).

State v. Fisher, 318 N.C. 512, 531–34, 350 S.E.2d 334, 345–47 (1986) (rejecting defendant's argument that counsel was ineffective in this murder case by admitting malice during closing arguments without defendant's consent; counsel never clearly admitted guilt; additionally, there was no ineffectiveness under *Strickland*).

State v. Perez, 135 N.C. App. 543, 547–52, 522 S.E.2d 102, 106–08 (1999) (counsel was not ineffective by conceding to the jury in opening and closing arguments that defendant was responsible for the death and was guilty of some offense less than first-degree murder where there was a "clear record" of defendant's consent to the admission; counsel's concession of defendant's guilt was a reasonable trial strategy to pursue imperfect self-defense), *review denied*, 351 N.C. 366, 543 S.E.2d 140 (2000).

State v. Watkins, 89 N.C. App. 599, 607–09, 366 S.E.2d 876, 881–82 (1988) (rejecting defendant's argument in this rape and sexual offense case that counsel was ineffective by stating in closing argument without defendant's consent: "I think there was anal intercourse"; without citing *Harbison*, the court held that given the evidence of anal intercourse, counsel's statement was not prejudicial).[13]

[14]   Failure to Move to Arrest Judgment

State v. Lowery, 318 N.C. 54, 67, 347 S.E.2d 729, 738 (1986) (counsel was not ineffective by failing to request that the court arrest judgment on a conspiracy conviction; arresting judgment would not have been proper since the conspiracy conviction did not merge with the murder conviction).

State v. White, 87 N.C. App. 311, 322–23, 361 S.E.2d 301, 307–08 (1987) (rejecting defendant's claim that counsel was ineffective by failing to move for arrest of judgment on possession of stolen property convictions where trial court was not required to arrest judgment), *aff'd in part and rev'd in part on other grounds*, 322 N.C. 770, 370 S.E.2d 390 (1988), *abrogated on other grounds*, Horton v. California, 496 U.S. 128 (1990).

[15]   Miscellaneous Trial Claims

State v. Lesane, 137 N.C. App. 234, 246, 528 S.E.2d 37, 45 (2000) (counsel's mistaken understanding as to the punishment for first-degree murder was not deficient where the prosecutor and judge labored under the same misunderstanding; additionally, defendant suffered no prejudice).

§ 2.04   Ineffectiveness in Connection with Sentencing or Dispositional Hearing[14]

[1]   Failure to Move for a Continuance

In re **Clapp,** 137 N.C. App. 14, 25–26, 526 S.E.2d 689, 697–98 (2000) (juvenile's attorney at a dispositional hearing was not ineffective by failing to move for a continuance on grounds that the judge had not received sufficient social, medical, psychiatric, psychological, and educational information; juvenile failed to prove that counsel's performance fell below an objective standard of reasonableness and that he was prejudiced by the alleged deficient performance; counsel had successfully obtained two prior continuances to secure the juvenile's presence, filed a notice of appeal and a motion for appropriate relief, and vigorously represented the juvenile at the hearing on the motion for appropriate relief).

---

13. In *Watkins*, the defendant apparently did not argue that counsel's statement constituted per se ineffectiveness under *Harbison*. *See* 89 N.C. App. at 609, 366 S.E.2d at 882 ("Defendant contends that this unauthorized admission . . . undermined his credibility to the extent that defendant was denied a fair trial").

14. For cases addressing claims of ineffectiveness in connection with capital sentencing proceedings, *see infra* § 2.09.

[2]   Silence, Failure to Call Witnesses, or Failure to Make
      Arguments in the Defendant's Favor

State v. Davidson, 77 N.C. App. 540, 543–47, 335 S.E.2d 518, 520–22 (1985) (counsel was ineffective at sentencing by offering no argument in defendant's favor, making no plea for findings of mitigating factors, failing to argue for reduced punishment on the basis that defendant was not the armed participant, failing to suggest any favorable or mitigating aspects of defendant's background, failing to advocate leniency, and offering commentary "entirely negative to defendant"; the court stated: "A declaration which fails altogether to articulate the positive, stresses counsel's status as an appointed representative, and presents defendant in an entirely negative light, cannot constitute . . . effective representation . . . . [A]t the very least effective representation demands that counsel refrain from making negative declamations.").

State v. Swann, 322 N.C. 666, 688, 370 S.E.2d 533, 546 (1988) (counsel was not ineffective by failing to make an argument at the sentencing hearing; defendant was not prejudiced by counsel's conduct because he "effectively received the minimum possible sentence for his crimes").

State v. Strickland, 318 N.C. 653, 660–62, 351 S.E.2d 281, 285–86 (1987) (rejecting defendant's contention that counsel was ineffective at sentencing by offering no evidence in mitigation, failing to make any remarks, and failing to oppose the State's showing in aggravation; the sentencing hearing was very brief, counsel was not utterly silent, counsel did not err in failing to oppose the State's evidence in aggravation, defendant failed to bring forward any evidence of factors in mitigation that should have been presented at the hearing, and there was nothing to indicate that counsel's conduct was anything other than strategic; court was not convinced that even if counsel had highlighted the "positive" aspects of defendant's offense and urged the judge to impose presumptive sentences concurrently, there was a reasonable probability that different sentences would have been imposed).

State v. Montford, 137 N.C. App. 495, 502–03, 529 S.E.2d 247, 252–53 (counsel was not ineffective by failing to call any witnesses at defendant's sentencing hearing where counsel made short argument advocating lenient sentencing), *cert. denied*, 353 N.C. 275, 546 S.E.2d 386 (2001).

State v. Taylor, 79 N.C. App. 635, 636–38, 339 S.E.2d 859, 860–61 (1986) (counsel's complete silence during sentencing was "troublesome" but not deficient performance prejudicial to the defense where nothing in the record indicated that counsel's decision to remain silent was not a tactical one).

State v. Crain, 73 N.C. App. 269, 272–73, 326 S.E.2d 120, 123 (1985) (counsel was not ineffective by failing to subpoena character witnesses to mitigate the sentence; because defendant received the mandatory minimum, he was not prejudiced by counsel's failure to offer mitigation witnesses).

State v. Scober, 74 N.C. App. 469, 473–74, 328 S.E.2d 590, 592 (1985) (rejecting defendant's claim that counsel was ineffective by failing to argue factors in mitigation at the sentencing hearing where defendant failed to produce any evidence of factors in mitigation that should have been argued).

[3]   Miscellaneous Sentencing Claims

State v. Skipper, 146 N.C. App. 532, 536–37, 553 S.E.2d 690, 693 (2001) (because trial court did not violate G.S. 14–7.6 (statutory provision stating that the trial court may not use same conviction used to establish habitual felon status to enhance a defendant's sentencing level), counsel was not ineffective by failing to object to sentencing on those grounds).

§ 2.05   Ineffectiveness in Connection with Appeal[15]

State v. Chance, 347 N.C. 566, 567–68, 495 S.E.2d 355, 356 (1998) (rejecting defendant's argument that counsel was ineffective by failing to perfect an appeal and "improper[ly] prepar[ing]"; counsel did perfect an appeal and defendant did not specify what was improper about counsel's preparation).

State v. Lowery, 318 N.C. 54, 67, 347 S.E.2d 729, 738 (1986) (rejecting defendant's argument that counsel was ineffective by failing to appeal; counsel's failure to appeal was compensated for when the federal *habeas* court required a belated appeal).

§ 2.06   Conflict of Interest Claims

State v. James, 111 N.C. App. 785, 433 S.E.2d 755 (1993) (fact that court made no inquiry about conflict created by counsel's dual representation of defendant and

---

15. As noted above, the constitutional right to counsel on direct appeal of right is grounded in due process and equal protection. *See supra* Part I, note 2.

The United States Supreme Court has decided several claims asserting IAC in connection with appeal. In *Roe v. Flores-Ortega*, 528 U.S. 470 (2000), the Court summarized its holdings in this area. *Roe* noted that the Court had long held that when a lawyer disregards specific instructions from a defendant to file a notice of appeal, the lawyer's conduct is professionally unreasonable. *See id.* at 477 (citing Rodriquez v. United States, 395 U.S. 327 (1969)). The *Roe* Court noted that it also had held that a defendant who expressly instructs counsel not to file an appeal cannot later allege that counsel rendered deficient performance by following his instructions. *See id.* (citing Jones v. Barnes, 463 U.S. 745 (1983)). In *Roe*, the Court addressed a split between the circuits on whether counsel is deficient for not filing a notice of appeal when the defendant has not clearly conveyed his or her wishes one way or the other. It held that in order to evaluate the reasonableness of counsel's conduct in these circumstances, it must answer the preliminary question of whether counsel in fact consulted with the defendant about an appeal. If so, counsel renders deficient performance only by failing to follow the defendant's express instructions regarding an appeal. *See id.* at 478. If counsel did not consult with the defendant, the court must inquire whether the failure to do so was itself deficient performance. *See id.* On this point, the Court rejected a bright-line rule that counsel must always consult with the defendant regarding an appeal. *See id.* at 480. Instead, the Court held that counsel has a "constitutionally-imposed duty" to consult with the defendant about an appeal where there is reason to believe either (1) that a rational defendant would want to appeal or (2) that this particular defendant reasonably demonstrated to counsel that he was interested in appealing. *See id.* (providing additional guidance on the relevant determination).

a prosecution witness when counsel acknowledged the conflict during cross-examination of the witness was "in and of itself . . . reversible error"; court also found record clearly showed that the conflict adversely affected counsel's performance).

State v. Yelton, 87 N.C. App. 554, 559–62, 361 S.E.2d 753, 756–58 (1987) (holding that record clearly demonstrated that father and son codefendants represented by the same lawyer voluntarily, knowingly, and intelligently waived their right to appeal on grounds of conflict of interest and that the trial court erred by failing to accept their waivers and requiring that counsel represent only one of the defendants).

State v. Walls, 342 N.C. 1, 39–41, 463 S.E.2d 738, 757–58 (1995) (rejecting capital defendant's claim that his right to effective assistance of counsel was violated when the trial court failed to resolve an alleged conflict of interest created by defense counsel's prior representation of a prosecution witness; prosecutor, not defense counsel, raised the issue and the court conducted an "adequate inquiry"; even if defense counsel actively represented conflicting interests, defendant failed to establish that the alleged dual representation actually affected the adequacy of his representation).

State v. Bruton, 344 N.C. 381, 390–92, 474 S.E.2d 336, 343–44 (1996) (in a case where the trial court held a pretrial hearing on possible conflict arising from counsel's joint representation of codefendants and obtained a waiver of the right to separate counsel, the court rejected defendant's claim that an actual conflict arose at trial requiring mistrial; defendant failed to show that an actual conflict of interest adversely affected counsel's performance).

State v. Hardison, 143 N.C. App. 114, 120–21, 545 S.E.2d 233, 237–38 (2001) (rejecting defendant's conflict of interest claim where defendant's counsel indicated at the sentencing hearing that he had been personal friends with the victims for fifty years; defendant failed to establish that he was adversely affected by any friendship or acquaintance that his counsel had with the victims).

State v. Winslow, 97 N.C. App. 551, 556, 389 S.E.2d 436, 439–40 (1990) (rejecting drug codefendants' contention that conflict of interest stemming from multiple representation adversely affected counsel's performance because each defendant was precluded from defending with evidence that he possessed only some or none of the cocaine; because there was strong evidence that each codefendant constructively possessed all the cocaine, the court found that defendants were not "prejudiced by having one attorney who did not present these defenses").

State v. Brewington, 80 N.C. App. 42, 47–48, 341 S.E.2d 82, 85–86 (1986) (counsel represented defendant and a codefendant at trial; defendant, who made no objection at trial, failed to show that an actual conflict adversely affected counsel's performance; fact that victim identified only the codefendant did not create an actual conflict and defenses presented "were not antagonistic").

§ 2.07 Prosecution Conduct

State v. Grooms, 353 N.C. 50, 65–67, 540 S.E.2d 713, 723–24 (2000) (rejecting defendant's claim that the State's bad faith conduct in failing to timely inform defense counsel that DNA sample had been consumed in SBI testing resulted in a violation of his right to effective assistance; concluding that defendant could show neither deficient conduct nor prejudice), *cert. denied*, 122 S. Ct. 93 (2001).[16]

State v. Taylor, 340 N.C. 52, 63–65, 455 S.E.2d 859, 865–66 (1995) (rejecting defendant's argument that the State's failure to timely provide discovery and divulge exculpatory information violated his right to effective assistance where defendant ultimately received the requested information at trial, was allowed to explore his theory related to it, counsel competently and zealously argued this theory to the jury, and evidence of guilt was overwhelming; defendant failed to show prejudice).

§ 2.08   Denial of Counsel Claims

[1]   Limitations on Defense Counsel's Conduct or Ordering Defense Counsel to Engage in Certain Conduct

State v. Call, 353 N.C. 400, 413–15, 545 S.E.2d 190, 199–200 (rejecting capital defendant's claim that the trial court violated his right to effective assistance by permitting only one of his attorneys to object during the prosecutor's direct examination of a witness; holding that even if defendant had properly preserved the issue for appeal, it would fail because an indigent defendant's right to the appointment of *additional* counsel in capital cases is statutory, not constitutional), *cert. denied*, 122 S. Ct. 628 (2001).

State v. Bowman, 349 N.C. 459, 474–75, 509 S.E.2d 428, 438 (1998) (rejecting defendant's contention that he was deprived of effective assistance when the trial court sustained the prosecutor's objection to defense counsel's closing argument regarding his conception of reasonable doubt; the trial court properly sustained the prosecutor's objection to counsel's argument; even if the trial court erred in sustaining the objection, the error was cured when the court thereafter correctly instructed the jury on reasonable doubt).

State v. Frye, 341 N.C. 470, 492–93, 461 S.E.2d 664, 674–75 (1995) (rejecting capital defendant's claim that the trial court violated his right to effective assistance by allowing only one of his attorneys to conduct *voir dire*; concluding that even if the issue had been preserved for review, it would fail because "an indigent defendant's right to the appointment of *additional* counsel in capital cases is statutory, not constitutional") (quotation omitted).

State v. Buckner, 342 N.C. 198, 214–17, 464 S.E.2d 414, 423–24 (1995) (rejecting capital defendant's argument that the trial court violated his right to effective assistance by instructing the jury that it should disregard counsel's argument that the jurors should evaluate the evidence in light of the severity of the potential sentence; although trial court erred, error was not prejudicial where the jury "was well aware of the severity of the consequences of its verdict . . . as well as the punishments").

---

16. Although the *Grooms* court analyzed the defendant's claim under *Strickland*, the defendant alleged that state interference—not attorney error—resulted in a denial of the right to effective assistance. *See generally* LaFave, *supra* Part I, note 2, § 11.8.

State v. Ross, 329 N.C. 108, 112–17, 405 S.E.2d 158, 161–63 (1991) (rejecting defendant's argument that the trial court violated his right to effective assistance by directing defense counsel to prepare a statement affirmatively asserting a theory of self-defense and by later informing the jury venire that defendant was asserting self-defense; on the facts, neither the court's directive nor its statement to the venire prejudiced defendant).

State v. Smith, 320 N.C. 404, 415, 358 S.E.2d 329, 335 (1987) (defendant was represented by two lawyers at trial; the court rejected defendant's contention that the trial court deprived him of his right to effective assistance; the trial court had ruled that the defense attorney cross-examining a witness was the only one who could make objections on direct examination of that witness; the trial court acted within its discretion and defendant failed to show prejudice).

[2]   Denying a Defense Motion to Continue or Other Request for Additional Time

State v. Rogers, 352 N.C. 119, 122–26, 529 S.E.2d 671, 673–76 (2000) (granting capital defendant a new trial where co-counsel was appointed one day after lead counsel and only thirty-four days before the term of court during which the case was to be tried, the trial judge repeatedly denied counsels' requests for continuances, and counsel had insufficient time to prepare; presumption of prejudice applied).

State v. Pait, 81 N.C. App. 286, 290, 343 S.E.2d 573, 576 (1986) (defendant was denied effective assistance of counsel when he was indicted, arrested, had counsel appointed, was arraigned and pleaded guilty, and was convicted in one day; "because of the unusual celerity with which the State and court moved defendant's counsel was not, and could not have possibly been, prepared to effectively advise and assist his client as . . . [he was] appointed . . . to do").

State v. Walls, 342 N.C. 1, 23–25, 463 S.E.2d 738, 747–49 (1995) (capital defendant was not denied effective assistance when trial court denied his motion to continue made just before jury selection; defendant had adequate time to prepare his defense, had already been granted one continuance, had two investigators at his disposal and was granted additional funds to hire a third, counsel represented defendant's interests "vigorously," and the reasons advanced for the second continuance were "less than substantial").

State v. Tunstall, 334 N.C. 320, 328–32, 432 S.E.2d 331, 336–39 (1993) (defendant was not denied effective assistance when trial court denied his counsel's motion to continue based on the unavailability of defendant until the day before trial and the lateness of discovery provided by the State; defendant "totally failed" to establish that he was deprived of any constitutional right by a lack of a reasonable opportunity to consult with his attorney in preparation for trial; defendant did not show that having additional time to review the State's discovery would have enabled counsel to better confront the witnesses).

State v. Laws, 325 N.C. 81, 99–100, 381 S.E.2d 609, 620 (1989) (rejecting capital defendant's claim that his right to effective assistance was denied when the trial court refused to give defendant's counsel the weekend to prepare a closing argument for the guilt-innocence phase; counsel's closing met an objective standard of reasonableness and was within the range of competence demanded of attorneys in capital cases), *reversed on other grounds*, 494 U.S. 1022 (1990).

State v. Locklear, 322 N.C. 349, 356–57, 368 S.E.2d 377, 382 (1988) (rejecting capital defendant's claim that his right to effective assistance was violated when the trial court failed to intervene *ex mero motu* to continue a hearing on certain pretrial motions in order to provide court-appointed counsel "adequate time" to confer with retained counsel; holding that defendant had no constitutional right to the assistance of additional counsel in the hearing on his motions or otherwise).

State v. Covington, 317 N.C. 127, 129–30, 343 S.E.2d 524, 525–26 (1986) (rejecting defendant's contention that by denying his motion to continue when he first learned the names and addresses of all the State's witnesses, the trial court violated his right to effective assistance; defendant was not entitled to the names any earlier than they were provided and he failed to show how his case would have been better prepared had the motion been granted or that he was materially prejudiced by its denial).

State v. Ford, 314 N.C. 498, 502, 334 S.E.2d 765, 768 (1985) (trial court did not violate defendant's right to effective assistance by denying his motion to continue where motion to continue was based on State's change in dates of two alleged offenses; because defendant was acquitted of those offenses, no prejudice resulted from the denial of the motion to continue).

State v. Hill, 116 N.C. App. 573, 578–79, 449 S.E.2d 573, 576 (1994) (rejecting defendant's argument that his right to effective assistance was violated when the trial court denied his motion to continue to allow counsel time to prepare for DNA analysis evidence presented by the State; the trial court allowed defendant's motion for funds to hire a DNA expert, turned the State's report over to defendant and ordered that defendant's DNA expert have immediate access to all discoverable information, and continued the case for eight days to allow defendant adequate time to contact an expert and have the DNA testing and report evaluated; defendant failed to show error or prejudice).

State v. Bunch, 106 N.C. App. 128, 131–32, 415 S.E.2d 375, 377–78 (1992) (rejecting defendant's contention that the trial court violated his right to effective assistance by denying his motions to continue; counsel had approximately fifty-five days to prepare for trial, motions to continue did not indicate that any witnesses would be presented on defendant's behalf or that defendant would testify, State called only two witnesses at trial, defendant received copies of both witnesses' statements and counsel thoroughly cross-examined the witnesses, and defendant put on no evidence; trial court did not abuse its discretion in denying the motions and defendant failed to show prejudice).

State v. Williams, 100 N.C. App. 567, 570–71, 397 S.E.2d 364, 366 (1990) (rejecting defendant's argument that by denying his motion to continue the trial for eight days, the trial court deprived him of his right to effective assistance; although original counsel withdrew from the case, substitute lead counsel was appointed twelve weeks before trial, co-counsel was appointed more than three weeks before trial, and lead counsel began proceeding with discovery only days after his appointment).

State v. Brooks, 83 N.C. App. 179, 182–84, 349 S.E.2d 630, 633 (1986) (rejecting defendant's contention that by refusing to grant his motions to continue the trial, counsel was not given a reasonable time to investigate and prepare his case and thus he was denied effective assistance; defendant filed no affidavits in support of his motions and did not show that he was prejudiced by their denial or that counsel's performance at trial or before trial was deficient in any way).

State v. Duncan, 75 N.C. App. 38, 42–44, 330 S.E.2d 481, 485–86 (1985) (trial court did not violate defendants' right to effective assistance by denying their motion to continue where defendants failed to demonstrate prejudice; continuance was requested for service of subpoena on witness who would have provided only corroborative evidence).

[3] Failure to Subject the State's Case to Meaningful Adversarial Testing

State v. Dockery, 78 N.C. App. 190, 191–92, 336 S.E.2d 719, 721 (1985) (rejecting without expressly addressing defendant's claim that counsel failed to subject the State's case to meaningful adversarial testing).

[4] Miscellaneous Denial of Counsel Claims

State v. Davis, 353 N.C. 1, 14–17, 539 S.E.2d 243, 253–55 (2000) (rejecting defendant's argument that by refusing to disclose the exact content of communications from the jury while deliberations were under way, failing to let counsel see or read the notes, allegedly misrepresenting their content and responding without eliciting and considering the informed positions of defendant and his counsel, the trial court deprived defendant of his right to effective assistance; the trial judge made a fair and accurate disclosure of the contents of the notes and counsel had opportunity to object to the proposed instruction), *cert. denied*, 122 S. Ct. 95 (2001).

State v. Pittman, 332 N.C. 244, 261, 420 S.E.2d 437, 447 (1992) (rejecting defendant's contention that the trial court violated his right to effective assistance by refusing to hear his counsel's arguments in favor of his motion to suppress; defense counsel never made any effort to make argument in support of the motion and only indicated to the court that he had three cases discussing the State's burden on the motion, which the court declined to review).

§ 2.09 Issues of Ineffectiveness Unique to Capital Cases[17]

State v. Fletcher, 354 N.C. 455, 481–84, 555 S.E.2d 534, 550–51 (2001) (rejecting defendant's contention that by conceding, with defendant's consent, that the crime was heinous, atrocious, and cruel, counsel rendered deficient performance; given the "overwhelming evidence" on this issue, counsel's concession was not objectively

---

17. On November 18, 2002, the United States Supreme Court granted *certiorari* in a capital case that will require it to decide whether defense counsel was ineffective under *Strickland* by failing to investigate available mitigation evidence. *See* Wiggins v. Corcoran, 123 S. Ct. 556 (2002).

unreasonable; noting that *Harbison* does not apply at sentencing), *cert. denied*, 123 S. Ct. 184 (2002).

State v. Call, 353 N.C. 400, 413–15, 545 S.E.2d 190, 199–200 (rejecting capital defendant's claim that the trial court violated his right to effective assistance by permitting only one of his attorneys to object during the prosecutor's direct examination of a witness; holding that even if defendant had properly preserved the issue for appeal, it would fail because an indigent defendant's right to the appointment of *additional* counsel in capital cases is statutory, not constitutional), *cert. denied*, 122 S. Ct. 628 (2001).

State v. Grooms, 353 N.C. 50, 84–86, 540 S.E.2d 713, 734–35 (2000) (rejecting capital defendant's claim that he was deprived of his right to effective assistance of counsel when the court ordered defendant's counsel to acquiesce to defendant's wishes not to present mitigating evidence after the court found the defendant and counsel reached an absolute impasse on the issue), *cert. denied*, 122 S. Ct. 93 (2001).

State v. Peterson, 350 N.C. 518, 526–28, 516 S.E.2d 131, 136–37 (1999) (rejecting defendant's contention that by submitting to the jury the (f)(1) statutory mitigating circumstance (no significant history of prior criminal activity) over defense counsel's objection, the defense team's credibility was injured and it was saddled with an impossible mitigating circumstance that it could not defend, thereby violating defendant's right to effective assistance of counsel; because the mitigating circumstance was supported by the evidence, the trial judge was required to submit it regardless of defense objection; submission neither prejudiced defendant nor injured defense team's credibility before the jury), *cert. denied*, 528 U.S. 1164 (2000).

State v. Smith, 347 N.C. 453, 468–70, 496 S.E.2d 357, 366–67 (1998) (rejecting defendant's claim that by submitting to the jury the (f)(1) statutory mitigating circumstance (no significant history of prior criminal activity) over defense counsel's objection, he was deprived of his right to effective assistance of counsel; even if it was error to submit the mitigating circumstance, no extraordinary facts were present and thus the error, if any, was harmless).

State v. Sanderson, 346 N.C. 669, 684–85, 488 S.E.2d 133, 141 (1997) (counsel was not ineffective by failing to object to a jury instruction in the sentencing phase of a capital trial that allegedly prohibited jurors from considering mitigating circumstances which had not been unanimously found by the jurors; counsel's performance was not deficient because the instruction did not require the jurors to consider only those mitigating circumstances unanimously found; also, defendant failed to show that counsel's performance "deprived him of a fair capital sentencing proceeding").

State v. Heatwole, 344 N.C. 1, 13–14, 473 S.E.2d 310, 315–16 (1996) (a capital defendant, who pleaded guilty, sought a new sentencing proceeding contending that the State's alleged *Brady* violation rendered his counsel ineffective; the court rejected the defendant's contention, holding that no *Brady* violation occurred).

State v. Frye, 341 N.C. 470, 492–93, 461 S.E.2d 664, 674–75 (1995) (rejecting capital defendant's claim that the trial court violated his right to effective assistance by allowing only one of his attorneys to conduct *voir dire*; concluding that even if the issue had been preserved for review, it would fail because "an indigent defendant's right to the appointment of *additional* counsel in capital cases is statutory, not constitutional") (quotation omitted).

State v. Buckner, 342 N.C. 198, 214–17, 464 S.E.2d 414, 423–24 (1995) (rejecting defendant's argument that by instructing the jury to disregard counsel's argument that they should evaluate the evidence in light of the severity of the potential sentence, the trial court deprived him of his right to effective assistance; although trial court erred, error was not prejudicial where the jury "was well aware of the severity of the consequence of its verdict . . . as well as the punishments" and thus no prejudice resulted).

State v. Walls, 342 N.C. 1, 57–58, 463 S.E.2d 738, 768 (1995) (counsel did not admit capital defendant's guilt before a jury against defendant's wishes when arguing with regard to the (f)(1) mitigating factor (no significant history of prior criminal activity): "I'm not going to ask you to answer that 'yes' ladies and gentlemen"; defendant himself put evidence of his record before jury and "*Harbison* applies only to the guilt/innocence phase of a trial").

State v. Simpson, 341 N.C. 316, 358–59, 462 S.E.2d 191, 215–16 (1995) (rejecting defendant's claim that the standards for proportionality review are vague and arbitrary and deprived him of his right to effective assistance).

State v. Bacon, 337 N.C. 66, 90–92, 446 S.E.2d 542, 554–55 (1994) (rejecting capital defendant's claim that counsel was ineffective during resentencing by presenting videotaped depositions from defendant's former friends and neighbors containing references to his possible parole and by presenting evidence that defendant had received a death sentence in the first sentencing proceeding; counsel's conduct was not unreasonable).

State v. Locklear, 322 N.C. 349, 356–57, 368 S.E.2d 377, 382 (1988) (rejecting capital defendant's claim that his right to effective assistance was violated when the trial court failed to intervene *ex mero motu* to continue a hearing on certain pretrial motions in order to provide court-appointed counsel "adequate time" to confer with retained counsel; holding that defendant had no constitutional right to the assistance of additional counsel in the hearing on his motions or otherwise).

§ 2.10   Lack of Ability or Experience

State v. Bailey, 145 N.C. App. 13, 22–23, 548 S.E.2d 814, 820–21 (2001) (rejecting defendant's argument that counsel was ineffective by not limiting the extent of his representation pursuant to G.S. 15A-141 and "thereby rendering defendant vulnerable to the consequences of representation by inexperienced counsel"; defendant failed to establish any particular error committed by counsel that affected the outcome of the trial).

State v. Blackwell, 133 N.C. App. 31, 37–38, 514 S.E.2d 116, 120–21 (1999) (rejecting defendant's argument that he was denied effective assistance because one of his attorneys had only practiced for a few months; finding counsel's inexperience "of no consequence" where his actual performance did not fall below an objective standard of reasonableness).

§ 2.11   State Bar Disciplinary Action

State v. Blackwell, 133 N.C. App. 31, 37–38, 514 S.E.2d 116, 120–21 (1999) (rejecting defendant's argument that he was denied effective assistance because one of his attorneys was subsequently suspended from practice for reasons unrelated to defendant's case; the disciplinary action "was of no consequence" where counsel's actual trial performance did not fall below an objective standard of reasonableness).

State v. Edwards, 73 N.C. App. 599, 601, 327 S.E.2d 16, 17–18 (1985) (rejecting defendant's claim that counsel's pending and ultimate disbarment "raise[d] a reasonable doubt as to the effectiveness of his assistance at trial" where the disciplinary proceedings did not begin until after defendant's trial had ended; the court held that "[o]nly rarely will such surrounding circumstances justify a presumption of ineffectiveness independent of counsel's actual trial performance" and subsequent disbarment "does not appear to be such a circumstance"; "*subsequent* disbarment proceedings generally are irrelevant in considering Sixth Amendment claims") (emphasis in original).

§ 2.12   Miscellaneous Allegations of Ineffective Assistance of Counsel

[1]   Totality of Conduct Reveals Ineffectiveness

State v. Moorman, 320 N.C. 387, 392–402, 358 S.E.2d 502, 506–12 (1987) (ineffective assistance was established where counsel presented defense theories to the jury that had no foundation in his pretrial investigation and that were unsupported by evidence, and counsel regularly used a variety of painkilling drugs, had frequent migraine headaches, and was drowsy, lethargic, and inattentive during portions of the trial; "a reasonable probability is created that had all these things not occurred the trial outcome might have been different").

[2]   Claims Failing to Allege Specific Acts of Ineffectiveness

State v. Chance, 347 N.C. 566, 567–68, 495 S.E.2d 355, 355 (1998) (rejecting defendant's argument that counsel was ineffective because of "improper preparation" where defendant failed to specify what was improper about counsel's preparation).

State v. Jones, 97 N.C. App. 189, 202–03, 388 S.E.2d 213, 220–21 (1990) (rejecting defendant's claim that counsel was ineffective by "fail[ing] throughout the trial to present evidence and cross examine witness [*sic*] in a sufficient manner"; defendant did not indicate what evidence counsel failed to present or what matters he failed to inquire into on cross-examination; counsel vigorously opposed admission of damaging evidence).

[3]   Failure to Make Arrangements for the Defendant's Disability

State v. Atkins, 349 N.C. 62, 111–12, 505 S.E.2d 97, 126–27 (1998) (rejecting defendant's argument that "trial counsel's failure to investigate his hearing loss and take appropriate measures to protect his rights" denied him effective assistance; nothing in the record suggests counsel failed to deliver "an appropriate level of . . .

representation" and defendant presented no evidence indicating that he informed trial counsel that he was unable to hear).

[4]   Disclosure of Privileged Information

State v. McIntosh, 336 N.C. 517, 525, 444 S.E.2d 438, 442 (1994) (rejecting defendant's argument that counsel's disclosure of attorney-client privileged information constituted per se ineffectiveness where information was not privileged).

Table of Authorities

Federal Constitution and Rules

U.S. CONST. amend. VI,   1, 5
Federal Rule of Criminal Procedure 44(c),   38

Federal Cases

Abbatte v. United States, 359 U.S. 187 (1959),   15
Ake v. Oklahoma, 470 U.S. 68 (1985),   66
Alabama v. Shelton, 122 S. Ct. 1764 (2002),   7, 13, 14
Allen v. Barnes Hospital, 721 F.2d 643 (8th Cir. 1983),   5
Anders v. California, 386 U.S. 738 (1967),   23
Appel v. Horn, 250 F.3d 203 (3d Cir. 2001),   27
Argersinger v. Hamlin, 407 U.S. 25 (1972),   14
Arizona v. Fulminante, 499 U.S. 279 (1991),   51, 52
Baylor v. Estelle, 94 F.3d 1321 (9th Cir. 1996),   55
Bell v. Cone, 122 S. Ct. 1843 (2002),   23, 25, 26, 28, 29
Beets v. Scott, 65 F.3d 1258 (5th Cir. 1995),   39, 43, 44
Blockburger v. United States, 284 U.S. 299 (1932),   15
Brecht v. Abrahamson, 507 U.S. 619 (1993),   52
Brooks v. Tennessee, 406 U.S. 605 (1972),   24, 52
Burdine v. Johnson, 262 F.3d 336 (5th Cir. 2001),   6, 27
Burger v. Kemp, 483 U.S. 776 (1987),   38, 41, 42, 43
Campbell v. Rice, 265 F.3d 878 (9th Cir. 2001),   46
Caplin & Drysdale Chartered v. United States, 491 U.S. 617 (1989),   5
Chambers v. Maroney, 399 U.S. 42 (1970),   30
Chapman v. California, 386 U.S. 18 (1967),   50, 51
Childress v. Johnson, 103 F.3d 1221 (5th Cir. 1997),   26, 27
Coleman v. Alabama, 399 U.S. 1 (1970),   5, 10, 11, 52, 53, 54

State Constitution and Statutes

State Cases

Books and Articles

Subject Index